IT'S HISTORY
WITH THE
NASTY
BITS LEFT IN!

Scholastic Children's Books,
Euston House, 24 Eversholt Street,
London NW1 1DB, UK

A division of Scholastic Ltd
London ~ New York ~ Toronto ~ Sydney ~ Auckland
Mexico City ~ New Delhi ~ Hong Kong

Published in the UK by Scholastic Ltd, 2017

Text © Terry Deary, 2017
Illustrations © Martin Brown, 2017

Some of the material in this publication has previously been published in the *Horrible Histories* books © Terry Deary and Martin Brown 1993–2017/ *Horrible Histories*
Magazine 2012–2017

All illustrations © Martin Brown except:
pp.64–65 & p.114 © Philip Reeve: from *Incredible Incas*, 2000 & *20th Century*, 1996
pp.111–113 © Mike Phillips: from *Blitz*, 2009

ISBN 978 1407 18003 8

Printed and bound in the UK

2 4 6 8 10 9 7 5 3 1

CONTENTS

Terry Deary was born at a very early age, so long ago he can't remember. But his mother, who was there at the time, says he was born in Sunderland, north-east England, in 1946 – so it's not true that he writes all *Horrible Histories* from memory. At school he was a horrible child only interested in playing football and giving teachers a hard time. His history lessons were so boring and so badly taught, that he learned to loathe the subject. *Horrible Histories* is his revenge.

Martin Brown was born in Melbourne, on the proper side of the world. Ever since he can remember he's been drawing. His dad used to bring back huge sheets of paper from work and Martin would fill them with doodles and little figures. Then, quite suddenly, with food and water, he grew up, moved to the UK and found work doing what he's always wanted to do: drawing doodles and little figures.

This beastly bookazine belongs to:

- -

- -

- -

- -

KEEP OUT!

ALL ABOUT HORRIBLE YOU

I get asked a lot of questions about 'history' when I meet my readers. Now it's time to turn the tables and ask YOU those questions ... tell the truth or suffer the terrible *Horrible Histories* torture of being nibbled to death by ducks. Ready?

What is your favourite period in history?

Why do you like that period?

Who is your favourite character in history?

And why?

If you could bring anyone back to life who would you rather NOT meet from history?

If you could have a new *Horrible Histories* book then what would it be about?

And what would you call it?

HORRIBLE HISTORIES

draw your
cover here

TERRY DEARY

WHICH *HORRIBLE HISTORIES* CHARACTER ARE YOU?

Are you a rotten royal or a woeful warrior? Take the quiz and find out!

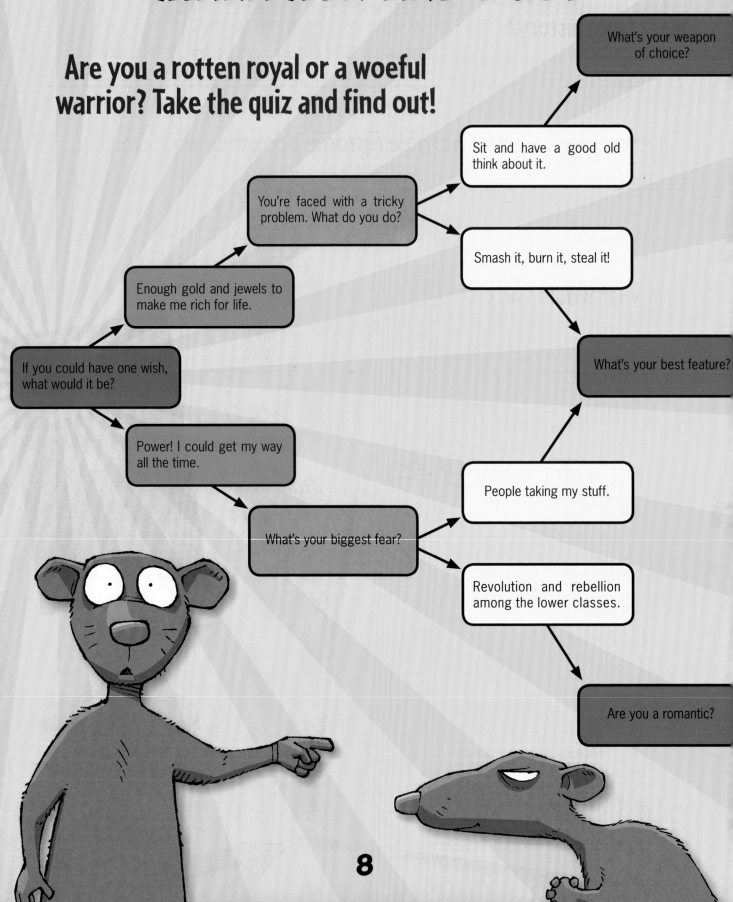

What's your weapon of choice?

Sit and have a good old think about it.

You're faced with a tricky problem. What do you do?

Smash it, burn it, steal it!

Enough gold and jewels to make me rich for life.

What's your best feature?

If you could have one wish, what would it be?

People taking my stuff.

Power! I could get my way all the time.

What's your biggest fear?

Revolution and rebellion among the lower classes.

Are you a romantic?

My razor-sharp mind and way with words. Has no one ever told you the pen is mightier than the sword?

You're WILLIAM SHAKESPEARE
You're the most famous playwright in history with a taste for truly gory stories. Some of the most horrible things to happen in your plays include eyes being ripped out on stage, live bears chasing people, mass murder and even cannibalism.

Swish, splat! You just can't beat a trusty axe.

You're THE EXECUTIONER
You're employed to chop the heads off lawbreakers and criminals. You've got a strong arm and a strong stomach, and you're not known for being particularly chatty! In fact, you've got a real air of mystery about you – dressed all in black and with a hood and mask over your face. Even your name is kept secret so no one will know you who are.

Long hair the colour of fire.

You're BOUDICA
Wow! It's not wise to get you angry. You're a Celtic queen who fought back hard when the Romans tried to take your land. You attack Roman settlements, burning them to the ground. One day you're finally defeated by a Roman general and you poison yourself.

A beard that makes me look extra fearsome.

You're A VICIOUS VIKING
You're brave, skilled with weapons and with a thirst for conquest. Very little scares you, and you'll go to any length to get what you want, even if it means stealing or killing. You've got a softer side too though, and you're great at carving and ship building.

Good grief no! I'm far too busy and important for such soppy things.

You're ELIZABETH I
You might be remembered today as the queen of a 'golden age', but you don't half have a bad temper. You hate to lose at anything and you make up nasty nicknames for your servants and courtiers. You never get married, and your death marks the end of the terrifying Tudors.

Yes, I fall in love all the time!

You're HENRY VIII
You're a powerful ruler with an enormous appetite – for power, for food and for wives for that matter! You have six wives during your lifetime, and a nasty habit of divorcing them or having their heads cut off! The only thing bigger than your heart is your belly.

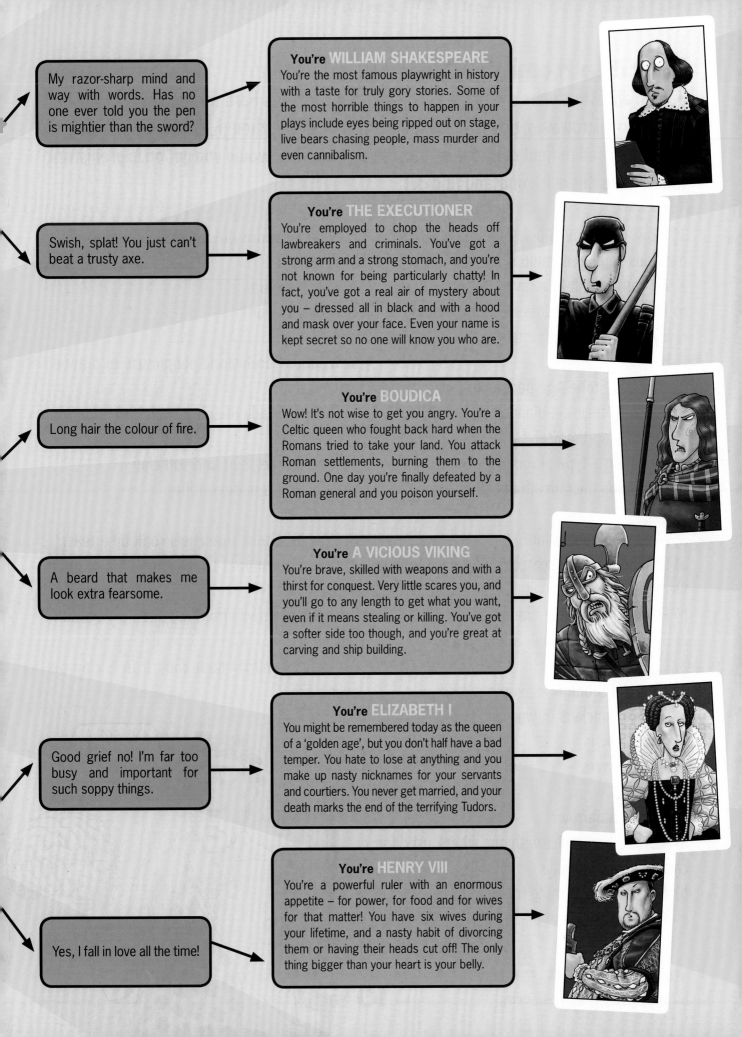

Horrible Hominid Quiz

Human ancestors were a strange bunch, but then, life was hard for hominids – they had no TV, no microwaves, no MP3 players (no school either, though, so maybe it wasn't so bad). They had to fight daily dangers just to survive. How would you get on in prehistoric times? Take this quick quiz and find out.

1. How did early Stone Age hunters trap a delicious woolly mammoth for their tea?
a) By cornering it in a cave
b) By stampeding it into a swamp
c) By tempting it with a teacake

2. How did Stone Age people go into a trance to talk with their dead ancestors?
a) By starving themselves
b) By eating a type of fungus
c) By holding their breath until they turned blue

3. What was trepanning?
a) Drilling a hole in someone's skull while they were alive
b) Dancing in a circle around a fire
c) Skinning a bison with a flint

4. What did Stone Age people wear?
a) Thermal knickers (it was cold in the Ice Age)
b) Animal skins
c) Woven leaves

5. What is a barrow?
a) A Stone Age device with one wheel, used for carrying dead animals
b) A Stone Age farming tribe
c) A Stone Age burial place

6. What weapons did Stone Age hunters use?
a) Flint axes
b) Machine guns
c) Wooden swords

7. What did prehistoric people use to draw on cave walls?
a) Brushes made of animal hair and juice from different fruit
b) Their fingers, flint and soft clay
c) Paint and a padded roller

8. How did Stone Age chefs cook up a feast?
a) Throw an animal in the fire – fur, feathers and all
b) Order takeaway from the pizza cave around the corner
c) Skin an animal then cook it in a clay pot over a fire

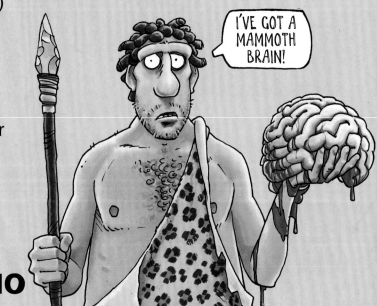

I'VE GOT A MAMMOTH BRAIN!

FOUL FOOD

Stone age humans couldn't pop down to their local supermarket and then shove food into their microwave ovens. Everything they ate had to be found or caught. If they wanted it cooked they had to do it themselves.

Tasty tips for hungry house-husbands and weary wives

You will need:
x dead animals- enough to feed the family
x a stone knife
x a flint to strike a light and wood for a fire

Methods:
1. Catch a bird or animal. (Handy hint: hang around beasts of prey like lions. Wait till they've eaten their fill and take what's left -but make sure they don't make a snack of you!)
2. Light the fire and build it up to a good blaze. (Handy hint: once you've got a fire going it is a good idea to try and keep it going until you need it again.)

3. Throw the dead animal on to the fire and scorch it till the fur (or feathers) burns off and the skin is crisp.
4. Pull the animal off the fire, slit it open, take out the guts and throw them away.
5. Tear off flesh and share it round the family. The meat will still be raw and bloody but don't worry, that makes it all the tastier.
6. Serve with fresh water.

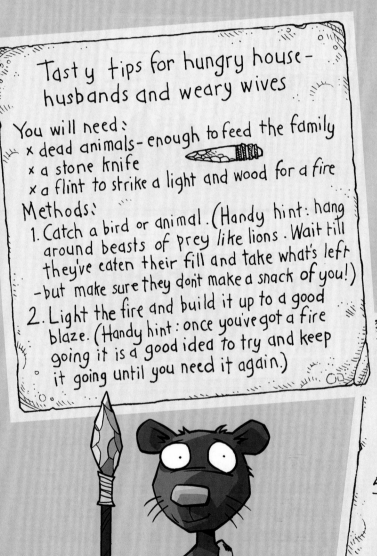

HORRIBLE HENGE

Everyone has heard of Stonehenge – those creepy-looking stones in Wiltshire have been around since prehistoric times. There have been some strange ideas throughout the ages about what they were used for, but which one of these weird and wacky theories is true?

A

STONEHENGE IS ABOUT THE SAME AGE AS THE PYRAMIDS, SO IT MUST HAVE BEEN BUILT BY EGYPTIANS

PROFESSOR E.X. PERT

B

STONEHENGE WAS BUILT BY PRIESTS FROM A MEDITERRANEAN ISLAND IN 1600 BC

PROFESSOR BRIAN STORM

C
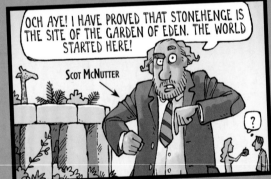

OCH AYE! I HAVE PROVED THAT STONEHENGE IS THE SITE OF THE GARDEN OF EDEN. THE WORLD STARTED HERE!

SCOT McNUTTER

D

STONEHENGE WAS BUILT BY ALIENS AS A LAUNCH PAD FOR THEIR SPACE SHIPS

N.E. JIT

Answer: None!

Archaeologists can explain how Stonehenge was built in the days before cranes and bulldozers. They've experimented with raising stones using ropes and wood. They can tell you *when* it was built and show how it was used to look. But they *can't* agree on what happened inside the stone circle. Guess it'll have to remain a mystery for now then.

Stonehenge is not the only stone circle in the British Isles – they are everywhere. Many stone-circle legends say the stones were once people or animals. Others say the stones were...

A complete wedding party, turned to stone for dancing on a Sunday
(Stanton Drew, Avon, England)

Three women who sinned by working on a Sunday (Moelfre Hill, Wales)

Giants who refused to be christened when Christianity came to the land
(Western Isles of Scotland)

Women who gave false evidence that led to a man being hanged
(Cottrell, South Wales)

A girl running away from a wizard who wanted to marry her
(Aberdeen, Scotland)

A cow, a witch and a fisherman (Inisbofin, Ireland)

A giant and his seven sons who went to war with a wizard (Kerry, Ireland)

A mermaid's children (Cruckancornia, Ireland)

Lots of places said the stones were robbers caught stealing from churches, or history teachers who gave impossibly hard homework and were turned to stone by pupils with witch powers ... you wish!

PYRAMID PUZZLER

Ancient Egyptians are famous today for building pyramids. They used them as places to bury their dead kings, in tombs filled with gold and other goodies.
Did you know...?

Around 100 pyramids have been discovered in Egypt.

Each pyramid needed about 25,000 men to build it.

A pharaoh called Khufu ordered his builders to create the biggest pyramid of them all. It used over 2.3 million blocks of stone, and some of them weighed nearly 14 tonnes!

Khufu's finished pyramid is called 'The Great Pyramid' and it's one of the Seven Wonders of the Ancient World.

Even though lots of history books have written about the pyramids, no one really knows how those awesome Egyptian people built them!

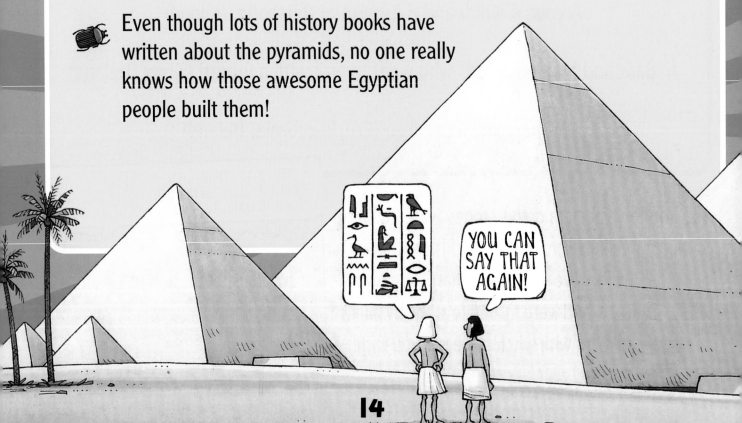

YOU CAN SAY THAT AGAIN!

Look at the pyramid below and see if you can find the hidden words. They could be listed forwards and backwards, across and diagonally. You can find the answers at the back of the bookazine.

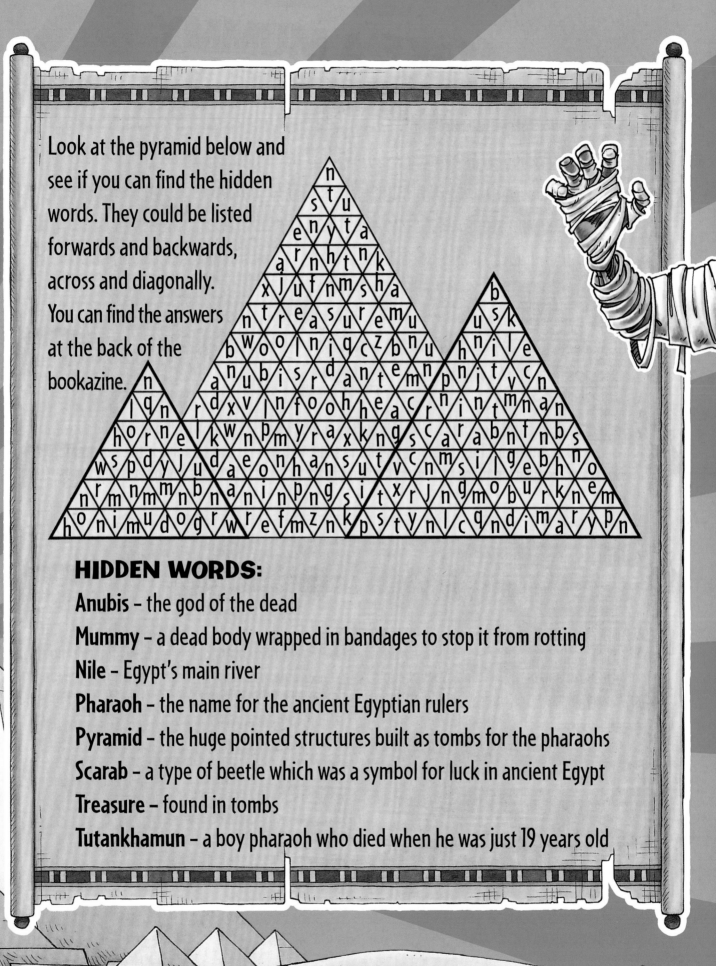

HIDDEN WORDS:

Anubis – the god of the dead

Mummy – a dead body wrapped in bandages to stop it from rotting

Nile – Egypt's main river

Pharaoh – the name for the ancient Egyptian rulers

Pyramid – the huge pointed structures built as tombs for the pharaohs

Scarab – a type of beetle which was a symbol for luck in ancient Egypt

Treasure – found in tombs

Tutankhamun – a boy pharaoh who died when he was just 19 years old

MAKE A MUMMY

The ancient Egyptians believed in life after death. To make sure they would get to the 'afterlife' they had to stop their dead bodies from rotting. Dead rich people were cleaned and wrapped in bandages. This is called 'mummification'. Read the mad mummy-making steps below and see if you can put them in the right order. The answers are at the back of the bookazine.

A – Rip open the front of the body, take out the insides, but leave the heart in place.

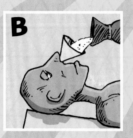

B – Throw the brains away and fill the skull with a type of salt.

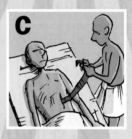

C – Stuff the empty body with rags to give it the right shape, then sew it up.

D – Take the body to a tent in the fresh air to blow away all the bad smells.

E – Wash the liver, stomach, guts and lungs in wine and put them in containers called canopic jars.

F – Put the body on a table with bars of wood so you can reach underneath to bandage it.

G – Open the mouth, or the mummy won't be able to speak or eat in the next life!

H – Soak the body in salt called natron for 70 days.

I – Wrap the body in bandages from head to toe.

J – Remove the brain through the nose with a big hook.

GRUESOME GODS

There were two sorts of gods in Egypt – the great gods that looked after the whole country – and the little gods that looked after your house and family.

Here are some of the groovy gods you could have prayed to in ancient Egypt.

Anubis

Looks like: a man with the head of a jackal (or a dog).
God of: the dead.

> Priests sometimes wore Anubis masks during the mummification process.

Hathor

Looks like: a woman with cow ears, or a cow or a woman with horns and a sun disc on her head.
Goddess of: music, dancing and beauty.

> A really stinky type of perfume called 'myrrh' was often used when praying to Hathor.

Looks like: an ape, or a man with the head of a frog.
God of: the air, and king of all the gods.

His nickname was 'The Great Honker' because he honked like a goose.

Horus

Looks like: a hawk or a man with the head of a falcon.
God of: the sky, protector of the pharaoh.

Horus lost his eye in a battle, but it was given back to him. This eye became a symbol of protection in ancient Egypt.

Osiris

Looks like: a mummified man with green skin.
God of: the Underworld and farming.

Legend says that the awful Egyptians used to be cannibals before Osiris taught them how to harvest grain.

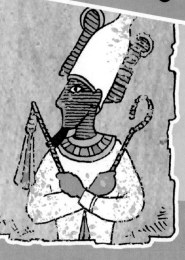

There are 11 differences between these two awful images – can you spot the lot? Answers at the back of the bookazine

QUEEN CLEO

The last great queen of Egypt was called Cleopatra. Read her savage story, and then colour in the picture of cool queen Cleo opposite.

Cleo was probably not a beautiful woman. She had a long hooked nose and a thick neck. She was clever though, she could speak nine languages! She took the throne when she was about 17 years old, then married her brother, Ptolemy, who was about 12. Yuck!

In 48 BC, the great Roman, Julius Caesar, landed in Egypt. Cleo had a long carpet rolled out for him, and she was wrapped up in it. Surprise, Caesar! Cleo and Caesar fell in love. Ptolemy ran away when he saw his sister making friends with his enemies. He drowned in the Nile as he fled.

When Julius Caesar died, Cleo married new Roman leader Mark Antony. Mark Antony was attacked by a Roman army and defeated. He blamed Cleo. To escape his anger she locked herself in her treasure house and sent him a message, 'Cleopatra is dead.'

Antony heard Cleo was dead. He was so unhappy he stabbed himself in the stomach and had himself carried to her treasure house. Cleopatra laid Antony on her bed but he died in her arms. Poor Cleo ordered a feast, and a man brought a basket of figs. There was a venomous snake hidden in the basket. Cleo pressed the snake to her arm. It bit her and she died on her golden bed. That was the end of the last queen of Egypt.

GRUESOME GREEK QUIZ

Simply answer 'Yea' for yes or 'Nay' for no to these facts about the grisly Greeks.

1 In the story of Troy, King Agamemnon sacrifices his daughter to the gods. Would that have really happened in ancient Greece?

2 A slave called Aesop told great stories such as 'The Tortoise and the Hare'. He was richly rewarded by the Greek priests.

3 The people who lived in the city of Sparta were super-tough kids. One Spartan boy hid a stolen fox cub under his tunic and didn't let on, even though the fox ate the boy's guts away.

4 In Draco's Athens (c. 600 BC) the laws were strict and you could be whipped for stealing a cabbage.

5 Athens' ruler Peisistratus (605–527 BC) arranged to have himself attacked so the people would feel sorry for him.

6 Teacher Socrates taught his students not to believe in the old Greek gods. Socrates was hanged.

7 General Alcibiades (450–404 BC) wanted people to notice him. Once he cut off his dog's tail to get a bit of attention.

8 The Greeks read the future using the guts of dead birds.

9 Hecate was the Greek goddess of crossroads. Greeks left food at crossroads for her.

10 The Greeks painted the doors of their houses red with blood.

Suffering Spartans

The Spartans were the toughest of all the Greek peoples – and it was extra-tough for Spartan kids. Here's a Spartan rule book with some of the words missing. Get the answers right – or take a savage Spartan punishment!

The missing words, in the wrong order, are: no clothes, hair, herd, thistles, mountains, whipped, baths, girls, bite, beaten

WHAT DO THEY SAY?

IN THE FUTURE THERE WILL BE FEWER BIRDS

1 A bad serving-child will receive a _____ on the back of the hand.

2 A sickly baby will be taken to the _____.

3 A new bride must cut off her _____ and dress like a man.

4 Children caught stealing food will be _____.

5 A child belongs to the state of Sparta. At the age of seven children will join a _____.

6 A Spartan child may have only a few _____ a year.

7 In processions, dances and temple services girls must wear _____.

8 If a Spartan child is cold in winter, then they may sleep under _____.

9 Good Spartans are _____ at the altar of the goddess Artemis.

10 _____ are to be trained for fitness by running, wrestling AND throwing quoits and javelins.

Answers at the back of the bookazine

OLYMPUS, GREECE, 776 BC
FIRST OLYMPIC GAMES

The ancient Greeks enjoyed games. Their cities battled against each other for prizes. The first Olympic Games were probably held in 776 BC ... and they could become quite gory games. If you want to run a REAL Olympics here are the rules...

OLYMPIC RULES

1 Naked men only. Women and girls are banned. They can't even watch.

2 Women who sneak in will be executed by throwing off a cliff. Don't even think about it, girls.

3 There are running, jumping and throwing contests. Relay races with flaming torches. A sports arena is one 'stadion' long (190 metres).

4 There is chariot racing as well as music, speaking and theatre contests for the not-so-fit.

5 Winners get crowns made from wild olive branches.

6 The winners at the Isthmian games are given a crown of CELERY as a prize.

7 The winner's name will also be called out to the crowds. You'll be famous.

8 Winners get free meals for life and pay no more taxes ... ever.

9 In 'pancration' wrestling you can strangle, kick, twist and even jump up and down on your opponent. How much fun is that?

10 Cheats will be fined – you have to buy an expensive statue to the god Zeus. So cut out the cons.

Those four-horse chariot races could be deadly dangerous. The poet, Homer, described an accident...

Eumelos was thrown out of the chariot beside the wheel. The skin was ripped from the elbows, nose and mouth, and his forehead smashed in over the eyebrows. His eyes filled with tears and his powerful voice was silenced.

The modern Olympics aren't so much fun.

GROOVY GREEK GAMES

Greek children invented games like knucklebones that are still played in some parts of the world today. In fact you may even have played some of the games yourself. If you haven't, and want to play like a groovy Greek, then here are the rules for six games.

OSTRAKINDA

This is a game for two teams that is still played in Italy, Germany and France.

You need: A silver coin. Paint one side black with poster paint – this side is 'Night'. The plain side is 'Day'.

Rules:

1 Divide into two teams – the 'Nights' and the 'Days'.

2 Spin the coin in the air.

3 If it lands black side up then the Nights chase the Days – and if it lands silver side up the Days chase the Nights.

COOKING POT

Rules:

1 Choose someone to be 'It'.

2 'It' is blindfolded and sits on the ground.

3 The others try to touch or poke 'It'.

4 'It' aims to touch one of the teasers with a foot.

5 Anyone touched by a foot becomes 'It', is blindfolded and sits on the ground.

BRONZE FLY

A sort of Greek Blind-man's Buff. A Greek described it...

They fastened a head-band around a boy's eyes. He was then turned round and round and called out, 'I will chase the bronze fly!'

The others called back, 'You might chase him but you won't catch him.'

They then torment him with paper whips until he catches one of them.

EPHEDRISMOS

Rules:

1 A player is blindfolded and gives a second player a piggy-back.

2 The rider then has to guide the player to a target set on the ground.

3 If the player succeeds then he becomes the rider. This could become a competition where pairs race to reach the target.

GREECKET

The Greeks also played ball games where you throw a ball at a 'wicket', rather like cricket without a batsman. We just have pictures of these games that have been painted on Greek vases, but we don't have their written rules. Make up your own rules – maybe they played like this...

1 Stand on a mark a fixed distance from the wicket.

2 Take the ball and have ten attempts to hit the wicket.

3 The opponent stands behind the wicket (like a wicket-keeper) and throws the ball back to you every time.

4 Then you stand behind the wicket while your opponent has ten tries.

5 The one who has the most hits of the wicket from ten throws is the winner.

6 Try again from a different mark.

It looks (from the vase paintings) as if the loser has to give the winner a piggy-back ride.

KOTTABOS

Rules:

1 Take a wooden pole and stand it upright.

2 Balance a small metal disk on top of the pole.

3 Leave a little wine in the bottom of your two-handled drinking cup.

4 Grip the cup by one handle, flick the wine out and try to knock the disk off the top of the pole.

(Would you believe grown-up Greeks played this silly game at parties?) You can try this with a cup and water and a 50p coin on the end of a broom handle ... but not in your dining room, please.

DUBIOUS DOCTORS

IF YOU LIVED IN ANCIENT GREECE YOU SHOULD NOT EVEN THINK ABOUT FEELING POORLY. DOCTORS WERE EVEN MORE DISGUSTING THAN YOUR BROTHER'S DIRTY SOCKS!

What's up, Doc?

The earliest Greek doctor was said to be called Aesculapius. But, since he was supposed to be the son of a god, he probably didn't exist.

But his followers, the Asculapians, did exist. They didn't work from a hospital, they worked from a temple. Most of their patients recovered with rest, sleep and good food. But Asculapians liked people to think they were gods so the patients had to say prayers and make sacrifices.

The temple was famous because no one ever died in the temple of Aesculapius and his doctor-priests! How did they manage this?

They cheated. If someone was dying when they arrived then they weren't allowed in. And if they started dying once they got inside they were dumped in the nearby woods.

I'M FEELING A LOT BETTER!

The doctor-priests were in it for the money. They warned patients that if they didn't pay, the gods would make them sick again. And they advertised. Carvings in the ruins show the doctor-priests made fantastic claims…

LAST WEEK A ONE-EYED MAN CAME TO THE TEMPLE. WHILE HE SLEPT THE GODS RUBBED OINTMENT ONTO THE EYELID, HE WOKE UP WITH TWO EYES.

SPECIAL OFFER AT THE TEMPLE – TWO FOR THE PRICE OF ONE

A SPARTAN GIRL, ARETE, SUFFERED FROM WATER ON THE BRAIN. AESCULAPIUS SIMPLY CUT OFF HER HEAD AND DRAINED THE WATER OFF. HE THEN CLEVERLY STITCHED THE HEAD BACK ON

BRILLIANT… UNFORTUNATELY HE STITCHED ON THE WRONG HEAD

HERAMUS OF MYTILENE WAS BALD. HIS FRIENDS MADE FUN OF HIM. WHILE HE SLEPT AESCULAPIUS RUBBED OINTMENT IN HIS HEAD. HERAMUS WOKE UP WITH A THICK HEAD OF BLACK HAIR

JUST REMEMBER TO GIVE IT A BOWL OF MILK EVERY DAY – AND KEEP AWAY FROM MICE

Horrible Hippocrates

Hippocrates (460–357 BC) was a Greek doctor who believed in the proper study of the body using experiments.

Hippocrates was so great that today's doctors still take the Oath of Hippocrates (though it has been altered in modern times) and promise:

I will give no deadly medicine to anyone if asked ... I will use treatment to help the sick but never to injure.

Hippo took samples from his patients and tested them. But he couldn't test them in a laboratory with chemicals the way modern doctors can. He tested them by tasting them or by making his patient taste them. But which of the following horrible things were tasted to test? Answer 'Yummy yes' or 'Nasty no'...

1 toenails
2 vomit
3 hair
4 ear wax
5 pus from infected wounds
6 tears
7 skin
8 snot
9 spit
10 pee

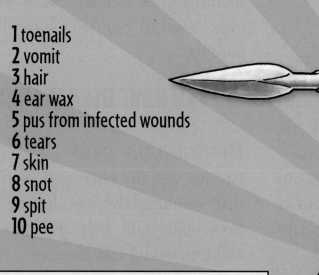

Answers:
1 Nasty no; 2 Yummy yes; 3 Nasty no; 4 Yummy yes;
5 Yummy yes; 6 Yummy yes; 7 Nasty no; 8 Yummy
yes; 9 Nasty no; 10 Yummy yes.

Next time you feel poorly why not take a bottle of pee and snot along to your doctor and ask him to taste it?

GRUESOME GREEK LEGENDS

Before the groovy Greeks came the mighty Mycenaean people, who ruled Greece. Their greatest palace was on the island of Crete – it was so posh the queen had the world's first flushing toilet. Then the palaces were wrecked and the Mycenaean way of life went too. No more flushing toilets. What went wrong? Was it…

• war and attack from outside?
• earthquakes?
• disease and plague?
• drought and famine?
• change of climate?

They've all been suggested by historians. But, like the disappearance of the dinosaurs, no one really knows for sure.

The *Dorian* people moved down into Greece. They forgot how to write so we don't know a lot about those days. Historians call them the *Dark* Ages.

DARN! HALF WAY THROUGH A LETTER AND I'VE FORGOTTEN HOW TO WRITE

So, without writing, the history was preserved in stories. And, as the years passed, the stories became wilder and more unlikely. Legends, in fact. The Greeks loved horror stories best of all. One Greek writer said that Greek children should not be told stories like this one (just as grown-ups today say you should not watch certain horror films).

But this bookazine is a horrible history and this story has a PG rating.

Do *not* read this story if you suffer from nightmares or at least read it with your eyes closed so you don't suffer the most gory bits.

YOU HAVE BEEN WARNED!

BRINGING UP BABY
Cronos was the chief god. You'd think that would make him happy, but no. Somebody told him that one of his children would take his place.

'Can't have that,' Cronos complained. 'Here, Mrs Cronos, pass me that baby!'

'What for?'

'Never mind daft questions. Just pass me that baby.'

Mrs Cronos passed across their new-born child. 'Here! What you doin' with that baby?' she cried.

'Eatin' it.'

'Eatin' it! You great greedy lummock. You've just had your tea. You can't be hungry again already.'

'I'm not hungry,' the great god growled. 'Just there's this prophecy about one of my children taking my throne. No kid, no take over, that's the way I look at it.'

'You don't want to go takin' no notice of them horry-scopes,' Mrs Cronos sighed.

'Don't pay to take chances is what I always say,' Cronos said smugly. 'Pass them indigestion tablets.'

Time passed, as time does, and Mrs Cronos had more baby gods … and Cronos ate every last one. Well, not the very last one. Mrs Cronos was getting fed up with his gruesome guzzling. 'I'll put a stop to his little game,' she smirked as she hid the new baby, Zeus, under her bed. She picked up a big rock, wrapped it in a baby blanket and dropped it in the cot.

In walked Cronos. 'Where is it?'

'In the cot.'

'Ugly little beggar, isn't he?' the head god said, squinting at the boulder.

'Takes after his father then,' Mrs Cronos mumbled.

'Crunchy as well,' her husband said, swallowing teeth.

'Probably cos he's bolder than the rest,' Mrs Cronos agreed.

Cronos sat down heavily on a royal couch. 'Ooooh! I think I've eaten someone who disagrees with me.'

'It's possible,' Mrs Cronos sniffed. 'A lot of people disagree with you, sweetheart.'

'Ooooh!' The god groaned and clutched his stomach. 'I think I'm going to be sick!'

'Not on the new carpet, my love. There's a bowl over there,' Mrs Cronos warned him.

Cronos gave a heavenly heave and threw up not just his stony snack, but all the other baby gods as well. 'Just goes to show,' Mrs Cronos smiled happily. 'You can't keep a good god down!'

And did the young gods grow up to overthrow their dreadful dad? What do you think?

ROTTEN ROMAN ARMY

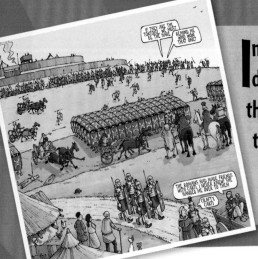

In the year AD 43 the Romans invaded Britain. The Roman Army didn't run all of Roman Britain. Once they'd won the battles they moved on to fight somewhere else. Towns were built in the beaten bits with Roman lords in charge.

Your teachers will tell you all about the legions and what they wore and how they lived. But they don't know everything.

TEST YOUR TEACHER...

Test your knowledge of what life was really like in the rotten Roman Army. You'll find the answers at the back of the bookazine.

If you were a Roman soldier...

1 What would you wear under your leather kilt?
a) nothing
b) underpants
c) fig leaves

2 Where would you drive on the Roman roads?
a) on the right
b) down the centre
c) on the left

3 How long would you have to stay in the army once you joined?
a) 25 years
b) 5 years
c) the rest of your life

4 Who could you marry?
a) your granny
b) no one
c) a Roman

5 Who paid for your uniform, weapons, food and burial?
a) the emperor
b) your granny
c) you paid for them yourself out of your wages

6 How tall did you have to be?
a) over 1.8 metres
b) between 1.6 and 1.8 metres
c) tall enough to touch your toes

7 What would you use instead of toilet paper?
a) a sponge on the end of a stick
b) your tunic
c) the daily newspaper

8 Your spear (pilum) had a 60 cm metal head that would snap off after it hit something. Why?
a) so the enemy couldn't pick up the spear and throw it back
b) so you could put the metal head in your pocket when you were marching
c) because the Roman armourers couldn't make the heads stay on

9 Why was one Roman Centurion called 'Give me another'?

"GIVE ME ANOTHER!"

a) because he liked his soldiers to sing as they marched. When they'd finished one song he'd call out, 'Give me another!'
b) because he was greedy. After eating a pig's head he'd cry out, 'Give me another!'
c) because he cruelly beat his soldiers so hard he smashed his canes and had to call out 'Give me another!'

10 Why would the army doctor not notice your screams as he treated your wounds?
a) because he enjoyed making you suffer
b) because he was trained to carry on without caring about a soldier's cries
c) because the Romans only employed deaf men as doctors

Answers at the back of the bookazine

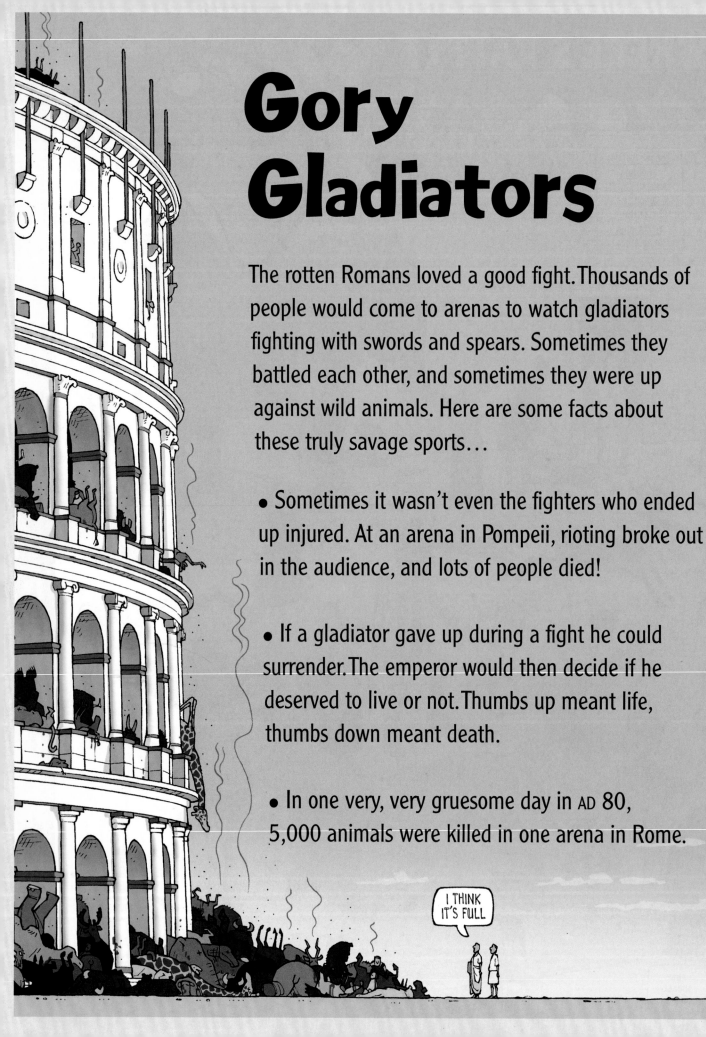

Gory Gladiators

The rotten Romans loved a good fight. Thousands of people would come to arenas to watch gladiators fighting with swords and spears. Sometimes they battled each other, and sometimes they were up against wild animals. Here are some facts about these truly savage sports…

• Sometimes it wasn't even the fighters who ended up injured. At an arena in Pompeii, rioting broke out in the audience, and lots of people died!

• If a gladiator gave up during a fight he could surrender. The emperor would then decide if he deserved to live or not. Thumbs up meant life, thumbs down meant death.

• In one very, very gruesome day in AD 80, 5,000 animals were killed in one arena in Rome.

I THINK IT'S FULL

Use your cruellest coloured pens to decorate this gladiator's shield.

FOUL FEASTING

Throughout history there have been some people who ate far more than anyone else. Far more than they needed to eat. Far more than an average person could eat. These sad people are known as gluttons.

In ancient history gluttony was 'good' – it showed the world how wealthy you were. Feasts were a way of showing off – the way rich people these days buy flashy cars. (BMWs hadn't been invented in ancient times.)

Kings, like Henry VIII of England and Louis XIV of France, were famous for their huge meals. But there were foul feasters many years before those kings. Here are a few tasty samples...

CALIGULA (ROMAN EMPEROR)

Said to have enjoyed drinking pearls dissolved in vinegar and to have served his guests with loaves and meats made out of gold. To entertain his guests, Caligula had criminals beheaded in the dining room as they feasted. (And some people still like a nice chop for dinner.)

VITELLIUS (ROMAN EMPEROR)

Known as 'The Glutton'. Said to have enjoyed three or four banquets a day. At one, his brother served up 2,000 fish and 7,000 birds. Fave recipe: pike livers, pheasant brains, peacock brains, flamingo tongues and the spleen of eels.
His priests gave sacred cake to the gods. Vitellius couldn't resist pinching it for himself.

NERO (ROMAN EMPEROR)

Nero hired a 'glutton' – a huge Egyptian slave who ate everything he was fed. This was feast-time fun for Nero's guests. What Nero enjoyed most was watching his glutton kill a man and eat him.

DINNER

ROTTEN ROMAN CHICKEN

The Romans loved throwing banquets and stuffing themselves with things like dormice and snails till they were sick. But sometimes they cooked quite tasty things, like this chicken dish. They didn't make this recipe up – they learned it when they invaded North Africa.

Ingredients:
Chicken pieces (one for each person)
1/4 teaspoon of cumin powder
1/4 teaspoon of coriander seeds
Four dates (chopped into small pieces)
4 tablespoons of chopped nuts
2 tablespoons of honey
2 tablespoons of wine vinegar
1 cube of chicken stock (crumbled in a cup of water)
A pinch of pepper
1 tablespoon of cooking oil
A handful of breadcrumbs

1. Put the chicken pieces in a roasting dish.
2. Brush them with cooking oil, sprinkle them with pepper and cover the dish with cooking foil.
3. Roast the pieces at 350 degrees Farenheit, 180 degrees Celcius or gas mark 4 for 30 minutes.
4. While the chicken is roasting, put the other ingredients into a pan and simmer for 20 minutes to make the Numidian sauce.
5. When the chicken pieces are ready, put them on a serving dish and pour over the sauce.
6. Serve the chicken with vegetables – cabbages and beans are very Roman.

Don't like the sound of this dire dinner? Maybe you'd prefer one of these treats from the Middle Ages. (You'd only have eaten these if you were rich – if you were poor you'd have scraped by with some porridge and a few vegetables.)

Porpoise Pudding – stuffed porpoise stomach

Trojan hog – pig stuffed with birds and shellfish, then roasted

Deer-antler soup – singed antlers, chopped and boiled with wine

Cockentrice – back half of a pig sewn together with front half of a chicken and roasted

Coqz Heaumez – whole roast chicken dressed in helmet and lance, sitting on a roasted hog (as if the hog was a horse)

Mashed deer tongues – served on fried bread

Roast peacock – skinned then roasted, then put back in skin so it looks alive

Pickled puffin – a puffin cooked and soaked in vinegar

Curried head – a warrior's head cooked in curry sauce (that's what Richard I of England ate during the Crusades)

BOUDICA
(died AD 61)

The Romans invaded Britain and took over the south – the bit we call England now. Some of the old Brit kings and queens fought to free themselves – queens like Boudica.

Famous for …

… revolting! The Romans robbed Boudica's Iceni tribe and flogged her. So in AD 61 she gathered an army and fought back. Her tribe attacked the Roman camps and murdered all the men, women and children they found there.

FOUL FACTS

✹ Boudica was extra cruel to the Roman women. She pushed a pointed pole through many of them, then hoisted them up to die.

✹ The Romans met the Iceni in a battle, and the Iceni brought their families along to watch. The families watched from a line of wagons at the back. The Romans drove Boudica's fighters back to the wall of wagons. The trapped fighters and their families were slaughtered: 80,000 Iceni died but only 400 Romans.

✹ Boudica didn't want to be a Roman slave so she took poison and died. Some say her body lies under Platform 8 of King's Cross Station in London.

Potty poem

Red-haired, angry, wild and mean,
Bou-di-ca the warrior queen.
Slaughtered Romans in their beds,
Lost in battle. Poison. Dead.

COLOUR IN BOUDICA

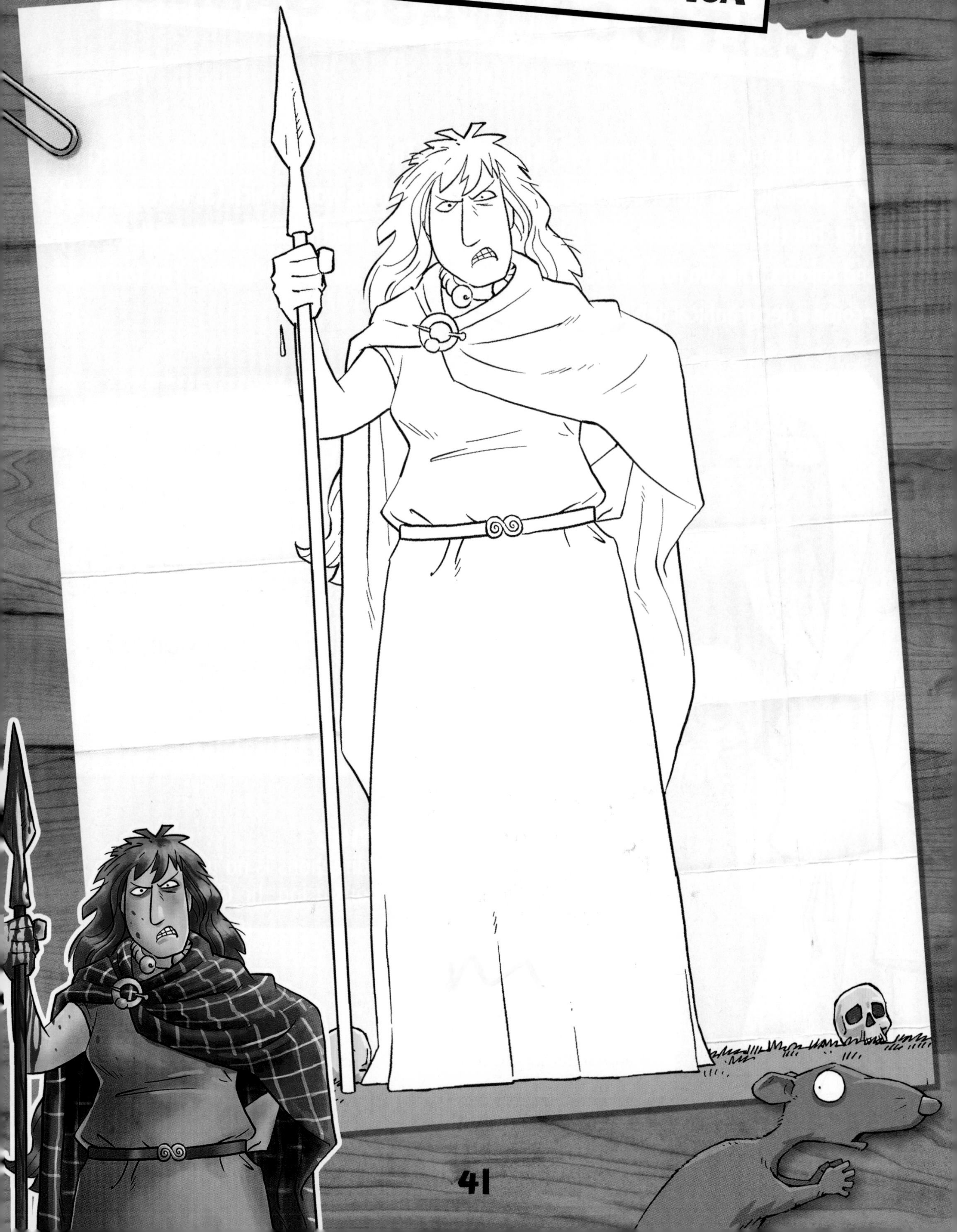

CELTIC COMPASS GAMES

Did you know that the Celts were skilful sailors? They needed a good sense of direction – after all, they didn't want to sail over the edge of the world which (as we can all see) is flat. But the Celtic sailors didn't describe directions as North, South, East or West. They used colours. The sun rose in the 'purple' and by midday was in the 'white'. You too could become a geographical genius by learning this chart...

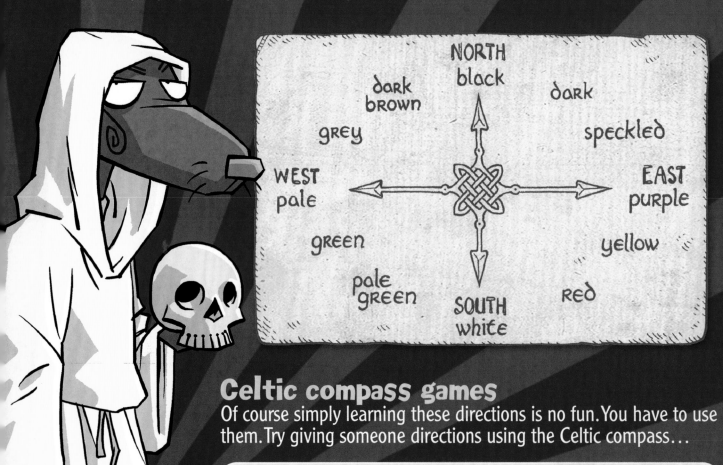

Celtic compass games

Of course simply learning these directions is no fun. You have to use them. Try giving someone directions using the Celtic compass...

Game 1
You'll need:
- ten or more players
- four signs saying North, South, East and West

All you do is:

1 Place the cards on each of the four walls of a large room or hall.

2 There is one 'caller' and the rest are runners.

3 The caller selects a colour – say, 'white' – and shouts it.

4 The players have to run to the correct sign – in this case 'South'.

SHARON'S ALWAYS BEEN VERY COMPETITIVE AT GAMES

5 The last one to touch the South wall is out.

6 The game continues with one player dropping out each round. Obviously, the corners are the colours or shades between the main compass points. 'Dark' or 'speckled' means North-east.

7 The winner is the last player in. Change callers and start again.

8 When the players are getting faster then add a new call … 'Cut-throat!' This means 'Freeze'. Everyone who moves after the call is out.

Game 2

You'll need:

- at least two players
- a room full of obstructions (like chairs)
- a scarf for a blindfold

All you do is:

1 The aim is for the leader to get the blindfolded partner safely across the room to a target without bumping, breaking or even touching an obstruction in between. (It would also be nice if the blindfolded partner does not break a leg.)

2 The leader must talk the partner through the obstacles but can only use the Celtic compass to do so.

3 'Black' becomes straight ahead, 'white' is backwards, 'purple' is right and 'pale' is left. 'Dark brown' is a little to the left and 'grey' is more to the left and so on.

4 The leader cannot use the word 'Stop' (or left, right, ahead or back) but they can add the word 'Cut-throat!' meaning 'Stop!'

5 Score 10 for a clear run to the target; deduct a point for every obstacle touched.

6 Change the blindfold to the leader and try again. The winner is the one with the highest score as leader.

7 If there is more than one pair, then the pairs can race from one end of the room to the other. Touching any obstacle means the pair must go back to the start.

8 The winner is the pair to reach the far wall first. In the event of a tie the winner is the blindfolded partner with the fewest broken bones.

DREADFUL DARK AGES

WHAT HAPPENS IF YOU ARE LIVING IN THE DARK AGES AND DO SOMETHING NAUGHTY? TOP TIP: 'DO NOT GET CAUGHT.' OTHERWISE YOU MIGHT MEET AN AWFUL END...

The Dark Ages (around AD 400–1000) are sometimes thought of as 'lawless'. When the Romans left Britain, the Angles and Saxons invaded. Then the Vikings began to rampage around Europe murdering monks, flattening farmers, bashing babies and terrorizing towns. But the deadly Dark Ages did have their own methods of punishment…

ALFRED THE GREAT? I'M ALFRED THE BLOOMIN' MARVELLOUS!

Artful Alfred

King Alfred ruled Britain from 871 till 901. He took all the old laws and organized them into a new book of laws for the Saxons.

There were ways of finding out if a person was guilty of a crime. They were called 'ordeals'. If you passed through the ordeal you were innocent – but if you failed you were guilty … and you suffered from both the test and then a punishment.

1. Ordeal by cake: A special cake is baked. The victim has to swear, 'If I did this crime then may this cake choke me!' and eat the cake. Sounds harmless enough, but Earl Godwin was banished from England for disobeying the good King Edward – a year later Godwin returned and declared…

PEOPLE SAY I KILLED YOUR BROTHER. BUT, IF THAT IS TRUE, THEN MAY GOD LET THIS PIECE OF BREAD CHOKE ME.

ME AND MY BIG MOUTH!

A minute later Godwin was dead. He had choked on the piece of bread!

2. Ordeal by cold water: The accused is tied hand and foot. A rope is placed around them and they are lowered into a pool. If they sink then they are innocent ... and if they float then they are guilty. (This test was still being used in the 17th century to test people accused of being witches! More about that later...)

3. Ordeal by hot water: The accused must plunge a bare arm into a pot of hot water and pull out a stone at the bottom of the pot. The arm will then be bandaged for three days. At the end of three days the bandage will be taken off. If the arm is healed then they are innocent ... but, if there is still a scald, they are guilty and must be punished.

4. Ordeal by hot metal: The accused must grip a hot iron rod and walk with it for a set distance. Again the hand is bandaged for three days and the wound examined.

5. Ordeal by combat: If two people argue about who owns a brooch or a piece of land (or a stale cheese sandwich) then they have a fight. The winner of the fight is judged to be the lawful owner. Actually, this still goes on in schools today!

6. Ordeal by lot: Try this in your own classroom!

YOU NEED:

Three sticks labelled 'GUILTY', 'NOT GUILTY' and 'TRINITY'. (The sticks used in iced lollies are best.)
A treasure (at least 2p and maybe as much as 5p).

TO WORK:

1 Select three people to be 'suspects' and one to be the 'judge'.
2 The judge places the treasure on the table and turns his or her back.
3 One of the suspects steals the treasure.
4 The judge blindfolds each suspect in turn and asks each one to pick a stick.

The suspect then gives back the stick to the judge.

5 The verdict: a) Pick 'GUILTY' and you are guilty.
b) Pick 'NOT GUILTY' and you are free to go.
c) Pick 'TRINITY' and you must pick another stick.
6 Of course all three could pick 'GUILTY' or all three could be 'NOT GUILTY'. Hard luck, judge. Try again until you get just one guilty person.

Try it. Does it work? It's not as painful as trial by boiling water but you could be found guilty just by picking the wrong stick. Good idea for football matches though - better than a penalty shoot-out.

NAME THAT NORSEMAN

The people of the 11th century were often named after their appearance. These nicknames were usually invented long after the person died by medieval writers. (It probably would have been a bad idea to go up to a Viking and call him 'Mr Flatnose'.)

Can you spot the real names here?

1 Viking Chief, Thorkell the...
a) Tall
b) Thin
c) Thick-as-Two-Short Planks

2 Danish conqueror, Svein...
a) Fork-tongue
b) Forkbeard
c) Fork-and-Knife

3 Ethelred's son, Edmund...
a) Ironheart
b) Ironside
c) Iron-Me-Shirt

4 Strathclyde king, Owen the...
a) Bald
b) Hairy
c) Permed

5 Earl of Orkney, Sigurd the...
a) Stout
b) Slim
c) Stuffed

6 Archbishop of York, Wulfstan the...
a) Wolf
b) Fox
c) Yeti

7 Duke of Normandy, Robert the...
a) Saint
b) Devil
c) Slightly Naughty

SOMEHOW I THOUGHT CAMELOT WOULD BE BIGGER

8 King Knut's son, Harold...
a) Flatfoot
b) Harefoot
c) Five-Foot-Two

9 Norse king of the Irish, Sigtrygg...
a) Silkbeard
b) Squarebeard
c) Bottle o' Beard

10 Wife of King Harold, Edith...
a) Swantail
b) Swan-Neck
c) Swansbum

11 King of Norway, Magnus...
a) Barefoot
b) Bareback
c) Bear-Hug

If you were a Viking what do you think your Norse name would be?

My Norse name would be _____

the _____

What would your best friend's Norse name be?

_____

What about your pet's Norse name?

_____

OK ERIC, YOU'RE THE GREAT NAVIGATOR — WHERE'S THIS BLINKIN' MONASTERY THEN?

VICIOUS VIKINGS

NOBODY IS SURE WHY THE FARMERS OF DENMARK AND NORWAY LEFT THEIR HOMES IN THE 700s AND STARTED RAGING ROUND THE WORLD. BUT YOU DID NOT WANT TO BE ONE OF THEIR VICTIMS.

IVAR THE BONELESS (VIKING, DIED AD 873) VICTIM: KING AELLA

People like horror stories. But the stories aren't always true, even if the people in them really did exist.

 IT ALL STARTED WITH KING AELLA OF NORTHUMBRIA IN ENGLAND. HE KILLED MY DAD. HIS MEN PUSHED HIM IN A PIT OF VENOMOUS SNAKES.

SO, THEY SAY ME AND MY BROTHERS CAPTURED AELLA AND TOOK A TERRIBLE REVENGE. FIRST WE TIED HIM TO A TREE...

...THEN WE CUT HIS RIBS AWAY FROM HIS BACKBONE. VERY PAINFUL THAT ... DON'T TRY IT AT HOME.

REALLY OUCH

OUCH

THEN WE RIPPED OUT HIS LUNGS AND SPREAD THEM OVER HIS BACK LIKE THE WINGS OF AN EAGLE.

REALLY REALLY OUCH

REALLY REALLY DEAD

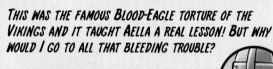

THIS WAS THE FAMOUS BLOOD-EAGLE TORTURE OF THE VIKINGS AND IT TAUGHT AELLA A REAL LESSON! BUT WHY WOULD I GO TO ALL THAT BLEEDING TROUBLE?

Thorgest thumped

The Vikings were supposed to be sneaky and use tricks like ambushes against their enemies. The Irish were supposed to be good sports who liked to fight fairly. But they didn't fight very fair when it came to getting rid of the first Viking chief, Thorgest.

Here's what happened…

Once upon a time there was a lovely Irish girl whose name we don't know.

So we won't tell you what it is.

Anyway, the Viking warrior Thorgest fell madly in love with the girl and he probably knew her name! 'Let's have a party in my castle tonight, lovely Irish girl. I'll bring a few of my warriors and you bring some of your lovely girl friends to keep them company,' Thorgest said.

'All right, Thorgest,' she said, 'But some of your friends are a bit rough and they'll scare my shy friends. Make sure they leave their weapons behind.'

'I will, lovely Irish girl,' Thorgest said.

So Thorgest turned up with a dozen of his warriors and the lovely Irish girl turned up with a dozen girls. The girls MAY have been lovely too but the Vikings couldn't see their faces. They were hidden behind veils. 'Right, lads,' Thorgest said, 'Start flirting!'

But when the Vikings walked up to the girls, the girls threw off their veils and their dresses!! Under those dresses they were Irish warriors with knives. They stuck the knives in the Vikings and killed them all except Thorgest.

The Viking leader was taken to Malachy, the king of Meath, who had him loaded in chains and drowned in a lake.

All because he fell in love with a lovely Irish girl whose name we don't know.

The End

Nice story, but probably just a legend. The massacre didn't do the Irish much good. More Vikings swarmed into Dublin to take thick Thorgest's place.

POTTY PROVERBS

The armies that invaded England brought with them terror, destruction, fear and ... language! The Viking invaders brought many words that we still use today.

These incredibly intelligent words of wisdom would not be possible if it hadn't been for the kindly Viking conquerors. Can you spot the three Viking words in each of these little-known Norse proverbs?

1 A flat egg on the plate is worth two in the dirt.

2 Bulls without legs give fewer steaks to the butcher.

3 Grubby kids with freckles don't look so mucky as those with plain faces.

4 Thieves who crawl low are not seen from high windows.

5 Reindeer with scabs give rotten meat to stew at Saturday suppers.

6 Dirty fellows become dazzling when washed with soft soap.

7 A knife in the guts will get even the grandest to gasp.

8 A score of scowling scarecrows will scare scamps.

9 Those who die meekly will receive no glittering crown in heaven.

10 Walk awkwardly and cruel people will scream and call you lame.

Answers:

1 Flat, Egg, Dirt
2 Bulls, Legs, Steaks
3 Kids, Freckles, Mucky
4 Crawl, Low, Windows
5 Reindeer, Scabs, Rotten
6 Dirty, Fellows, Dazzling
7 Knife, Get, Gasp
8 Score, Scowling, Scare
9 Die, Meekly, Glittering
10 Awkwardly, Scream, Call

QUICK VIKING QUESTIONS

Now find out if you're a vicious Viking expert with this quick Viking quiz.

1 The Danish Vikings had been invading England for centuries and some had settled – but they weren't popular. In 1002 the good folk of Oxford found a way to deal with the Danes who'd settled there. What way? (Clue: they liked to chop and change)

2 In 1004 the people of Norwich made a deal with the Vikings to stop the raids. What did they agree? (Clue: crime pays)

3 In 1006 King Ethelred of England was worried that his nobles were becoming too powerful. He had one noble, Aelfhelm of York, murdered. What did he do to make sure Aelfhelm's sons didn't rise up in revenge? (Clue: they didn't see the point)

4 By 1009 King Ethelred was desperate. He had paid fortunes to the Danes and they still raided and robbed England. What did he order his people to do? (Clue: oh my God!)

5 In 1010 a medical book of cures was printed, but not many people could read. They preferred old charms like 'Out little spear if you are in here.' What does that cure? (Clue: saves nine)

6 In 1014 Danish King Knut invaded Lincolnshire and took hostages. But when he was driven out by the English he didn't kill the hostages. What did he do? (Clue: a bit of this, a bit of that)

7 The Archbishop of Canterbury was captured by the Danes in 1012. He refused to pay a ransom so the drunken Danes pelted him with what? (Clue: they were feasting at the time)

8 Ethelred died in 1016 and councillors in Southampton elected Danish king Knut – while councillors in London elected English Edmund. Two kings for one kingdom? But Edmund came up with an easy solution. What? (Clue: dead easy in fact)

9 Knut became King of England in 1017. What did he do to the mother of his rival, Edmund? (Clue: knot a bad idea)

10 Eilmer the Monk broke both his legs in 1030. What was the mad man of God trying to do? (Clue: pigs might)

11 In 1040 Macbeth became King of Scotland. How did he kill the previous king, Duncan? (Clue: all's fair in love and...)

12 King Harthacnut accepted a drink from his half-brother and died in 1042. What sort of drink killed him? (Clue: half-brother gets the throne)

13 In 1054 King Macbeth of Scotland was beaten at the battle of Dunsinane. How long did he go on reigning after the defeat? (Clue: count Shakespeare's witches)

Answers at the back of the bookazine

THE NORMAN CONQUEST

HASTINGS, 14 OCTOBER 1066

Some Vikings moved south into France. The French king gave them a northern bit of his country just to keep them happy. These 'North-men' became the 'Normans'. One really fierce Norman, Duke William, started looking around for more land to conquer. He picked on England. In 1066, he landed on the south coast and met the English King Harold in battle at Hastings. He won.

It's England's most famous battle but how much do you know about it? Just answer 'True' or 'False'…

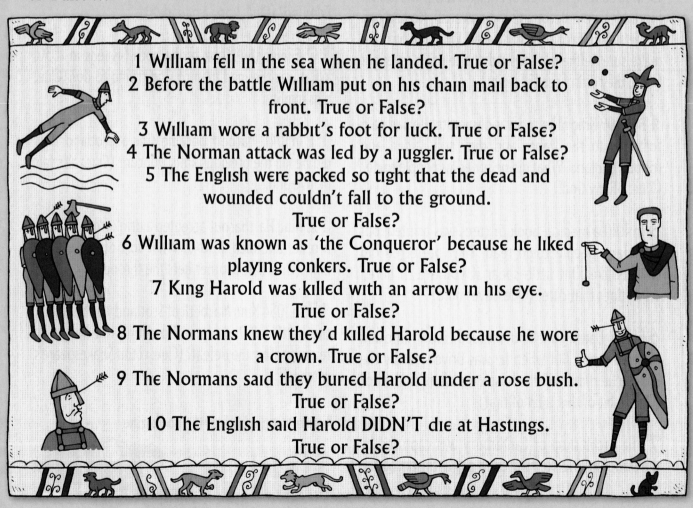

1 William fell in the sea when he landed. True or False?

2 Before the battle William put on his chain mail back to front. True or False?

3 William wore a rabbit's foot for luck. True or False?

4 The Norman attack was led by a juggler. True or False?

5 The English were packed so tight that the dead and wounded couldn't fall to the ground. True or False?

6 William was known as 'the Conqueror' because he liked playing conkers. True or False?

7 King Harold was killed with an arrow in his eye. True or False?

8 The Normans knew they'd killed Harold because he wore a crown. True or False?

9 The Normans said they buried Harold under a rose bush. True or False?

10 The English said Harold DIDN'T die at Hastings. True or False?

Answers

1 True. He stumbled and fell forward as he reached the beach. Ooops! His men gasped. A bad sign. But witty Will grabbed some pebbles, stood up and said, 'See how I have grabbed England?'

2 True. It was another unlucky sign. William just laughed and said, 'This is the day I "turn" from Duke to King.'

3 False. William wore the bones of Saint Rasyphus and Saint Ravennus around his neck for luck.

4 True. The Normans didn't want to attack up hill and risk their lives. At 9 a.m. the minstrel Taillefer began to juggle with his sword and sing a battle song. He attacked – an English warrior moved forward to meet him and Taillefer lopped off his head. Taillefer moved on – the English shields parted to let him through where they hacked him down. He died.

5 True.

6 False.

7 False. Harold was WOUNDED with an arrow to the eye. But he was KILLED when Norman knights charged forward and hacked him to bits.

8 False. Harold's face was smashed. Only his wife knew his corpse because she could spot its secret marks.

9 False. They said King Harold's corpse was taken to the sea shore and buried under a pile of stones. The English gave him a headstone reading, 'Harold, you rest here, to guard the sea and shore.'

10 True. The English told a story that Harold survived, buried under a pile of bodies. A peasant woman found him and nursed him back to health. He hid in a cellar in Winchester for two years before leading attacks on the hated Normans. In time he got religion and became Harold the hermit.

KNIGHTLY RULES

Knights had more rules than your school. It's true they didn't have *daft* rules like, 'Don't run in the corridor,' or 'Don't let the tyres down on the headteacher's car.' But they did have rules, like…

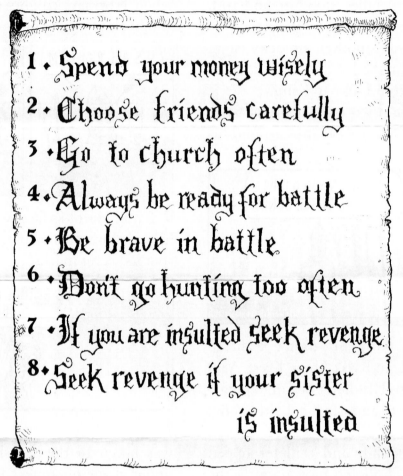

1 • Spend your money wisely
2 • Choose friends carefully
3 • Go to church often
4 • Always be ready for battle
5 • Be brave in battle
6 • Don't go hunting too often
7 • If you are insulted seek revenge
8 • Seek revenge if your sister is insulted

Some of these rules would be pretty difficult to follow nowadays (like spending your money wisely!) But some of the rules the knights believed we still use today. We have sayings like, 'Never kick a man when he is down.' How ridiculous! Who says you shouldn't kick a man when he's down? What better time is there to kick a man? If you kick him when he's standing then he might just kick you back.

We've labelled the rotten rules above from 1–8. Write the numbers into the below boxes in order of which ones you think would be easy to follow nowadays and which ones you think would be a tad trickier.

EASY PEASY ☐ ☐ ☐ ☐ ☐ ☐ ☐ ☐ **HORRIBLY HARD**

Dressed to kill

If you wanted to be a knight you had to dress to kill. But our terrific *Horrible Histories* researchers came across this knight who was dressed to be killed. We managed to make this sketch before the man-in-a-can started to go mouldy.

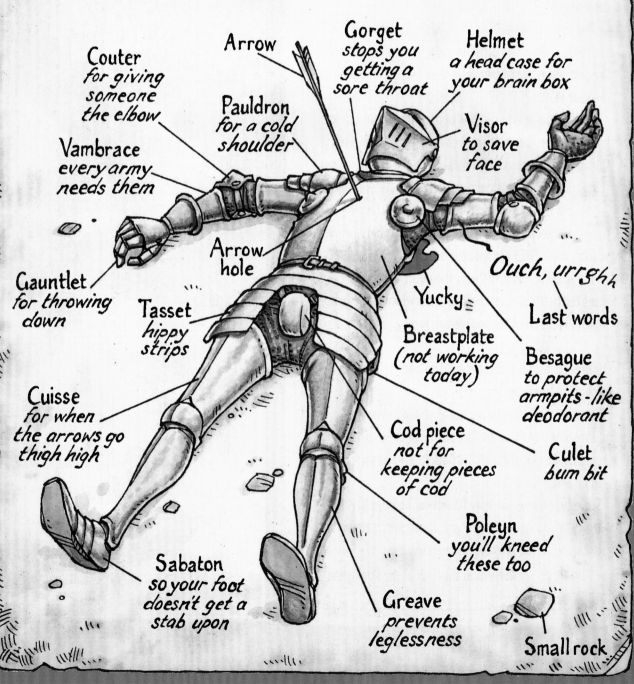

Couter
for giving
someone
the elbow

Arrow

Gorget
stops you
getting a
sore throat

Helmet
a head case for
your brain box

Pauldron
for a cold
shoulder

Vambrace
every army
needs them

Visor
to save
face

Arrow
hole

Ouch, urrghh

Gauntlet
for throwing
down

Yucky

Last words

Tasset
hippy
strips

Breastplate
(not working
today)

Besague
to protect
armpits - like
deodorant

Cuisse
for when
the arrows go
thigh high

Cod piece
not for
keeping pieces
of cod

Culet
bum bit

Poleyn
you'll kneed
these too

Sabaton
so your foot
doesn't get a
stab upon

Greave
prevents
leglessness

Small rock

CUTTER WHEY CASTLE

Some history books show you pictures of what a building might look like if it was 'cut away'. However, at *Horrible Histories*, the policy has always been to knock down a castle and REALLY cut it away.

We chose to vandalize Cutter Whey Castle in this way. We then invited our artist to draw the ruin and THEN imagine it was full of people as they may have looked in the year 1450.

Our illustrator is fairly good at drawing, as you can see, but happens to be pretty ropey when it comes to history. Our experts spotted TEN mistakes in the picture – ten things that would not be around in 1450.

We did think of sacking the artist and scrapping the painting, then we decided, 'No! Let the *Horrible Histories* readers see if THEY can spot the mistakes!'

If you think this is too easy then watch out! There are some red herrings – unexpected things which WERE in use in 1450. Well? What are you waiting for?

Score less than 5 and you should go back to a medieval school to be whipped.

Score 5, 6 or 7 and you are not as stupid as you look.

Score 8 or 9 and you are far too intelligent to be doing quizzes like this, show-off. Go back to a medieval school to be whipped.

Score 10? No one will score 10. Answer number 10 is too tricky. If you score 10 then you are almost certainly a cheat and a true *Horrible Histories* reader.

Answers at the back of the bookazine

BOOM!

CRAZY CURES

GOT A DREADFUL DISEASE? Here are a few top health tips from the putrid past. Just don't try them at home or on your friends. Try them on someone who won't be missed – a teacher perhaps?

CURES FOR TOOTHACHE

STONE AGE Eat hollyhock flowers.

SAXON Boil a holly leaf, lay it on a saucer of water, raise to your mouth and yawn.

STUART Scratch the gum with a new nail and then drive the nail into a tree.

GEORGIAN Burn the ear with hot poker.

CURES FOR SNAKE BITES

ROMAN Grind up fennel with wine and pour it in the nostrils, while rubbing pig droppings on the wound.

SAXON Get some wood from a tree grown in heaven and press it to the wound.

GEORGIAN Kill a chicken, rip out its guts and place them on the wound while still warm.

CURES FOR DIARRHOEA

ANCIENT EGYPTIAN Eat gruel, green onions, honey, wax and water. Yum.

INCA Chew coca leaves.

CURES FOR A HEADACHE

STONE AGE AND ROMAN Drill a hole in the skull.

SAXON Find some swallow-chicks, cut their stomachs open and look for some little stones. Tie the stones up in a small bag and put it on your head.

MIDDLE AGES Take off your hat so the harmful fumes can escape from your head.

INCA Gouge a hole between the eyes with a glass knife.

TUDOR Press a hangman's rope to the neck.

CURES FOR EYE PROBLEMS

ANCIENT EGYPTIAN Poor eyesight at night Eat roasted, crushed ox liver.

Cataracts Eat tortoise brain and honey.

Blindness Mash a pig's eye with red ochre and pour it into the ear.

SAXON Swollen eyelid Cut it out with a knife.

GEORGIAN Stye Rub it with the tail of a black cat.

CURES FOR BALDNESS

SAXON Burn bees and rub the ash on your head.

TUDOR Smear your head with fox grease, garlic and vinegar.

CURES FOR THE PLAGUE

MIDDLE AGES
- Wear a magpie's beak around your neck.
- Sit in a sewer.
- Drink ten-year-old treacle.
- Swallow crushed emeralds.
- Eat arsenic (a poison).
- Shave a live chicken's bottom and strap it to the plaguey sores.
- Move from town to town flogging yourself with a whip.

TUDOR Place a freshly killed pigeon on the sores.

CURES FOR A COLD

MIDDLE AGES Put mustard and onions up your nose.

VICTORIAN Wrap a sweaty sock around your neck.

CURES FOR FEVER

INCA For a baby Wash the baby in a bowl of its family's pee, and give it some to drink.

STUART Cut a pigeon in half and place one half on each foot.

CURES FOR GOUT (SWOLLEN JOINTS)

MIDDLE AGES Use a plaster made of goat droppings, rosemary and honey.

TUDOR Boil a red-haired dog in oil, add worms, pig marrow and herbs. Place the mixture on the affected area.

CURES FOR BRUISES

ROMAN Treat with unwashed sheep's wool, dipped in animal fat.

MIDDLE AGES Make a plaster out of bacon fat and flour.

CURE MOST LIKELY TO GET YOU LOCKED UP

Ambrose Pare, of France, was called a 'great' surgeon because he learned how to treat soldiers wounded in battle. But one of his ointments for a wound was just a little sick:

YOU NEED:
Two new-born puppies, 1/2 kg earthworms, 1 kg lily oil, 1/2 kg turpentine, 25 g of brandy.

TO MAKE:
Heat the oil and boil the puppies alive. Drown the earthworms in white wine, and add them. Boil and strain. Add the brandy and turpentine. Mix well. Rub the mixture into the wound.

SUFFERING SCHOOLS

In the Middle Ages in England and Wales it was tough at school.

Schools – the good news

* You didn't have to go if you were poor ... or a girl.
* Most boys only went to school from the ages of 7 to 14.
* There was no homework.
* There were no spelling corrections – you spelled English any way you wanted to.

Schools – the bad news

* You had no break-times – only a short stop for lunch.
* Make a mistake and you were beaten – usually with branches from a birch tree.
* You had to buy your own paper, ink and books – which were very expensive.
* And of course there were 'School Rules'…

Westminster School in the 13th century had the following rules...

Let them say prayers every morning without shouting

Let there be no grinning or chattering or laughing

Let them not make fun of another if he does not read or sing well

Let them not hit one another secretly

Let them not answer rudely if questioned by their elders

LET THOSE WHO BREAK THESE RULES FEEL THE ROD WITHOUT DELAY!

Not too bad so far? Not much different from your own school, apart from the bit about being hit with a rod!

Some of the other rules were really odd. But they must have needed these rules because someone actually did these dreadful deeds…

Anyone who has torn to pieces his schoolmate's bed or hidden the bedclothes or thrown shoes or pillows from corner to corner or thrown the school into disorder shall be severely punished in the morning.

No wonder this boy's 15th-century poem was so popular with pupils. He wrote about being late for school and giving a cheeky reply to his teacher...

My master looks like he is mad,
'Where have you been, my sorry lad?'
'Milking ducks my mother had!'
It is no wonder that I'm sad.

My master peppered my backside with speed,
It was worse than fennel seed;
He would not stop till it did bleed,
I'm truly sorry for his deed.

I wish my master was a hare,
And all his fat books hound dogs were.
Me, the hunter, I'd not spare
Him. If he died I would not care!

Why was the boy late? You might well ask. Well, school often began at five in the morning in summer time! Wouldn't you be late?

LOST PRUPERTY

Shoe
Sports kit socks

MUCKY MANNERS

Young people in the Middle Ages had books to teach them table manners. Unfortunately not a lot of young people could read. It may have been better to have had illustrations to help. Draw lines to match the putrid picture to the instruction it goes with. Number 2 is completed to show you how it's done.

Answers: 1)D, 2)G, 3)A, 4)I, 5)B, 6)H, 7)J, 8)E, 9)C, 10)F

1 DO NOT clean your nails or your teeth with your eating knife.

2 DO NOT wipe your knife on the tablecloth.

3 DO NOT play with the table cloth or blow your nose on your napkin.

4 DO NOT dip your bread in the soup.

5 DO NOT fill your soup spoon too full or blow on your soup.

6 DO NOT eat noisily or clean your bowl by licking it out.

7 DO NOT speak while your mouth is full of food.

8 DO NOT spit over the table but spit on the floor.

9 DO NOT tear at meat but cut it with a knife first.

10 DO NOT take the best food for yourself. Share it.

A

B

C

D

E

F

G

H

I

J

GRUESOME GRID

Copy the Middle Ages rat into the squares.

SCRAMBLED SAYINGS

The Irish, Scots and Welsh all have their own languages. But most people in Britain speak English most of the time.

They use the English language to say some pretty potty things – and some curiously clever things if you think about them.

Take the Irish in the Middle Ages. They had some puzzling sayings, like 'It's a bad hen that won't scratch herself' meaning people should be able to do their own work. That's useful when your mother tells you to go to the shop or do the washing up. (But not when your pocket money depends on it.)

Now you've got the idea, you should have no trouble putting the two halves of these Irish proverbs back together. Match the first column with the last. (Work out what they mean – or simply go around saying them, and everyone will think you're brilliant!)

1 A woman's tongue	a) speaks the truth
2 Death	b) is difficult to choose
3 The mouth of the grave	c) is better than a salmon in the sea
4 A trout in the pot	d) can lose his hat in a fairy wind
5 Even a tin knocker	e) does not rust
6 Between two blind goats it	f) is the poor man's doctor
7 Any man	g) will shine on a dirty door
8 When the tongue slips it	h) gives to the needy one

Answers at the back of the bookazine

INCREDIBLE INCAS

Inca Emperor Pachacuti decided it was time for some changes and he had the power to make them. He had only taken over as emperor from his father after a lot of fighting and he didn't want that to happen when he died, so he made his son Topa Inca Yupanqui the next emperor, then retired.

Topa was topa the pops when it came to ruling and he and his dad made some nice new rules. If the Incas had been able to write, their laws may have read something like this…

THE TEN INCA COMMANDMENTS

1. Cuzco will be the capital of the Incan Empire. The fortress of Sacsahuaman in Cuzco will be the strongest in the world.

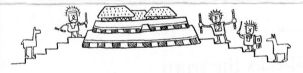

2. The people will work on improving the Cuzco valley farms – levelling the earth and moving the river – so it will be the greatest food producer ever.

3. A dead emperor's lands will be shared out amongst his family. Each new emperor must conquer new lands of his own.

4. Conquered peoples will be scattered round other parts of the Incan Empire to work for the Incas – that will also stop them gathering together to revolt.

5. Girls of conquered tribes may become Chosen Women (Quechua Aclla Cuna) to serve in the Incan temples or be married off to great Incan soldiers.

6. A number of conquered men will be chosen to serve in the Incan Army.

7. Everyone will worship the Incan god, Viracocha. There will be priests, prayers and temples. All conquered peoples must worship Viracocha, and pay his priests with food and work. (But they can keep their old religion too.)

8. The emperor may marry his sister, but no other men may marry their sisters.

9. The emperor may marry as many women as he wishes, but no other man may. A chief minister may have 50 wives, an ordinary minister just 30 and the lower your class the fewer wives you may have.

10. If anyone wishes to speak to the emperor then he or she must take off their sandals and place a small load on their back as a sign of respect.

WEE WOMEN

Girls! Want to look like an Incan woman? You'll need to dress your hair like the Incas. Here's how to do it...

1. Collect pee in a bucket. (Your family and friends can all chip in and help you fill that bucket fast.)

2. Leave the pee for a week to brew (the way beer is left to brew – except your pee won't end up tasting like brown ale).

3. Wash your hair by soaking it in the bucket of brewed pee. (This will get rid of the grease and leave your hair lovely and shiny – honest!)

4. When your hair is dry you can start making it into braids. To hold the hair in place wet it with some of that pee. (Hair spray hasn't been invented. Sorry.)

5. Find your Prince Charming and say...

Then hope that your Prince Charming likes a Cinderella who smells like a toilet!

IN MEXICO AROUND 1300 TO 1500 THE TERRORS OF THE TIME WERE THE AZTEC PEOPLE. OF ALL THE HORRIBLES IN HISTORY THE AZTECS COME CLOSE TO THE TOP OF THE PILE. JUST LOOK AT THEIR HORRIBLE HOBBY OF SACRIFICING HUMANS...

The good gore guide

You know that the sun is a star ... a large celestial body composed of gravitationally contained hot gases emitting electromagnetic radiation, especially light, as a result of nuclear reactions inside the star. (No, I don't understand what it means either but it sounds good if you say it quickly.)

Anyway the Toltecs believed it was actually a god. A superhuman being who has power over human life.

Now these god people can be very tricky. If you upset them then they'll make you suffer – shine too hot on your crops, shrivel them up and starve you, or send a plague of locusts to eat all your food. The thing to do is keep your god (or gods) happy.

Some people think their god will be happy with a bit of praise and a few hymns and prayers. Other people believe they have to give prezzies to their god.

The terrible Toltecs believed you had to give a life to their god – a sacrifice.

But the awful aztecs took it to extremes. They believed they had to give their sun god human lives – thousands of them. And, not only that, they had to be sacrificed in a gruesomely gory way.

The Aztecs didn't sacrifice the odd human on special occasions like the king's birthday or Bank Holiday Mondays. They did it all the time. They…

* sacrificed 50,000 a year (that's a thousand a week, six an hour or one every ten minutes!)
* sacrificed 20,000 in a single party when they opened the temple at Tenochtitlan.

* had an army specially organized to keep the priests supplied with victims.
* stirred up trouble among the conquered tribes so they had an excuse to go in and take prisoners who became sacrifice victims.

A Spanish history book said that when the Great Temple was opened in 1487 there were 80,000 victims sacrificed in one ceremony. But don't believe everything you read in history books! Because sacrificing 80,000 would have been just about impossible! The Aztecs would have needed machine guns and bombs to massacre that many. (In fact it's only in the past hundred years that humans have learned to kill each other at that rate – but modern people call it war and that makes it all right.)

BEASTLY BATTLE

In 1485 England was ruled by King Richard III. Ruthless Richard had his enemies (most kings did in those days), and these enemies looked around for someone to take Richard's place. They turned to an almost unknown Welshman called Henry Tudor.

Henry Tudor

Henry and Richard fought against each other in the Battle of Bosworth Field. Richard's friends deserted him and Henry won, becoming Henry VII, the first Tudor king.

Can you help Henry get through the maze to reach Richard and fight for the throne?

Richard III

Answers at the back of the bookazine

TERRIBLE TUDORS

Foul Family Facts

The Tudors were a family who ruled England, and poked their noses into the rest of Great Britain, from 1485 til 1603. The grandfather was Henry VII, his son was Henry VIII and the grandchildren were Edward VI, Mary I and Elizabeth I.

Five rulers and 118 years that changed the lives of the English people. Read on to find out who was who...

HENRY VIII
REIGNED: 1509–1547
MARRIED: Six times! Catherine of Aragon, Anne Boleyn, Jane Seymour, Anne of Cleves, Catherine Howard and Catherine Parr.
FOUL FACT: Henry reigned for 38 torturing Tudor years and, in that time, about 72,000 people were executed. That's about five every day.

HENRY VII
REIGNED: 1485–1509
MARRIED: Elizabeth of York
FOUL FACT: Henry was mean with his money. The gossips in the palace said the Queen had to borrow money from her servants.

EDWARD VI

REIGNED: 1547–1553

MARRIED: No one – he died at age 15, which didn't give him a lot of time.

FOUL FACT: In Edward's last days, his fingers turned black and dropped off and his hair fell out. Yeugh!

MARY I

REIGNED: 1553–1558

MARRIED: King Philip of Spain

FOUL FACT: Before she was queen, Catholic Mary pretended she wouldn't harm any Protestants. She lied! She killed over 300 once she was in charge.

LADY JANE GREY

REIGNED: 1553

MARRIED: Lord Guildford Dudley

FOUL FACT: Jane was queen for just nine days before she was arrested by Mary I and executed.

ELIZABETH I

REIGNED: 1558–1603

MARRIED: No one

FOUL FACT: After imprisoning her for 18 years, Elizabeth signed an order for her cousin, Mary Queen of Scots, to be executed. Not a close family then!

WICKED WORDS

It's said that Will invented about 1,705 new words in his writing ... someone with nothing better to do counted them! Look at the words in the book below and decide if you think each one was used first by Shakespeare. Write the word in the 'True' column if you think it was, and the 'False' column if you think it wasn't.

EYEBALL   BANANA   BLOODSTAINED
BUBBLEGUM   LONELY   RADIO

True

GLOOMY   ROLLERBLADE   JEANS
UNCOMFORTABLE

False

YE OLDE TUDOR WORD SEARCH

P	R	O	T	E	S	T	A	N	T	S	B	N	E	R
R	S	S	K	L	Y	R	N	E	H	J	P	P	X	I
F	H	P	P	L	V	R	P	F	F	O	H	L	N	Q
K	L	T	A	L	M	O	Z	E	P	I	J	I	J	K
F	M	T	O	N	P	I	O	F	O	E	N	C	R	L
L	W	R	L	A	I	D	F	L	H	R	C	E	D	F
E	Q	C	N	M	I	S	F	L	C	K	L	R	D	E
A	B	A	X	E	J	C	H	A	P	L	G	M	P	U
S	C	B	J	K	U	F	N	A	E	R	U	L	H	G
L	X	P	Q	M	E	P	L	Y	R	F	L	B	R	A
Y	U	I	C	R	W	Z	L	V	Z	M	A	M	I	L
T	N	D	O	Q	C	Z	Q	S	R	N	A	O	L	P
I	N	D	P	C	R	Z	B	Y	O	P	E	D	M	F
A	U	P	N	R	R	Y	P	M	D	F	B	N	A	H
T	D	Q	S	M	A	L	L	P	O	X	S	L	O	R

Shakespeare's just finished his new play — but he's missed out some words! Can you help him find them?

TUDOR
PROTESTANTS
SPANISH ARMADA
LICE
SMALL POX
PLAGUE
FLEAS
AXE
CHOP
HENRY

HE'S LOST FOR
WORDS?

Answers at the back of the bookazine

GROOVY GAMES WITH WICKED WORDS

People have always enjoyed playing word games. 'I spy with my little eye' is perfect for people with a great amount of time and a small amount of brain. But to really enjoy words you should try something a bit more challenging. Here are some wicked word games...

KNICKERS

For: Two or more players.
Rules: Dead simple. One player must answer every question with a single word each time ... choose a word like 'slime', 'snot', 'eyeballs' or something equally disgusting. However, if they laugh (or even give a hint of a Mona Lisa smile) they have lost.

Here's an example where the answer word is knickers...

Q: What do you wear on your head when you go to bed?
A: Knickers
Q: What do you call your cat?
A: Knickers
Q: What do you use to strain your tea?
A: Knickers

AMAZING ANAGRAMS

Mix up the letters of a word and spell a new word. That's an anagram. So t-a-m-e can become meat, mate or team.

Here are some clever anagrams you can bore your friends/ family/teachers with. Say, 'Did you know...?'

1 astronomer is an anagram of moon starer
2 schoolmaster is an anagram of the classroom
4 slot machines is an anagram of cash lost in 'em
7 punishment is an anagram of nine thumps

Got the idea? Then solve these anagrams (with the help of a clue) to give two famous names…

1 Hated for ill – he was hated because of what he did in the war!

2 Old west action – and he stars in films with plenty of that action.

PANGRAMS

If you can't manage an anagram then try a pangram. What has this sentence got?

Six crazy kings vowed to abolish my quite pitiful jousts

It is a pangram because it has all 26 letters of the alphabet in it. There are 47 letters in that sentence. Can you create a pangram with fewer?

ODDBOD BOYS

Is your name an anagram? Here are some sentences that contain mixed-up boys' names. Can you
a) find the boy's name then
b) untangle it? (Are you one of them?)

1 Here comes Slime.
2 Evil's his name.
3 He should be Nailed.
4 Larches is very wooden.
5 Lace is very rich.
6 Every school needs a Warden.

TO BE OR NOT TO BE, RAT IS THE QUESTION

REMEMBER, REMEMBER...

Since the Gunpowder Plot was discovered it has passed into English history and is remembered every 5 November. But how many of these funny Fawkes facts are false? Answers at the back of the bookazine.

1 In January 1606 Parliament passed a new law. It said that 5 November would become a holiday of public thanksgiving.

2 Guy Fawkes hasn't always been the one on top of bonfires. At different times in history dummies of different people have been burned on 5 November.

3 It wasn't until 1920 that fireworks were added to the 5 November celebrations.

4 For many years the people of Scotton village in Yorkshire refused to celebrate 5 November with fireworks and bonfires.

5 The government decided that the cellars beneath Parliament should be patrolled night and day to prevent another Gunpowder Plot. That patrol stopped a long time ago.

PENNY FOR THE GUY

GRUESOME GRID

Copy Guy Fawkes into the squares.

> 'THE BLACK DEATH' COULD KILL BY THE MILLIONS IN THE MIDDLE AGES. BUT THE PLAGUE WAS STILL JUST AS DANGEROUS IN THE TIMES OF THE SLIMY STUART MONARCHS OF THE 1600S.

Fire and plague

Londoners who lived through Charles II's reign were pretty lucky … lucky that the plague didn't get them! And if the plague spared their lives then the Great Fire probably destroyed their houses. Would you have survived in Stuart London?

The plague … read all about it!

PENNY FOR THE GUY

9th Sept 1665

PLAGUE WEEKLY
ON THE SPOTS REPORTS

Only 2OP WEEKLY

BOOZY BARD BEDEVILS BURIAL BOYS

Last night the brave burial boys, who collect your old corpses, were almost scared to death themselves. A strolling singer sat up and spooked them just as they were about to pop him in the pit.

DIRTY

Corpse collector Samuel Simple (34 or 37) said, 'It's a dirty job but somebody has to do it. We was going along picking up bodies off the doorsteps where their loved ones had dumped them. We came across this scruffy little feller in a doorway. The door was marked with a red cross or we wouldn't have taken him. Stuck him on the cart with the others and went off to the graveyard.'

His partner, Chris Cross (24-ish) added, 'We was just about to unload the cart when the bodies started moving, didn't they? Gave me a right turn, I can tell you. Turned out to be this singer trying to get out of the cart. What a mess. Bodies all over the place!'

SMELLY

Wandering minstrel Elwiss Prestley, of no fixed abode, said 'I'd had a few jars of ale and just sat down for a nap. Woke up under this fat, smelly feller. Thought it was somebody trying to muscle in on my sleeping spot. Told him to get off, didn't I? Course he didn't reply … well, he wouldn't, him being dead like.'

TONIC

Sam and Chris were able to laugh about their grave mistake. 'We'll buy Elwiss a drink to make up for it,' Sam said. 'We can afford it – after all, business is good at the moment. They're dropping like flies.' Asked how he stays so fit and healthy Chris said he put it all down to 'Doctor Kurleus's Cureall Tonic'.

Doctor Kurleus Cures All

This is to give notice that John Kurleus, former physician to Charles I, offers a drink and pill that cures all sores, scabs, itch, scurfs, scurvies, leprosies and plagues be they ever so bad. There is no smoking or sweating or use of mercury or other dangerous and deadly substances. Doctor Kurleus sells the drink at three shillings to the quart and the pill one shilling a box. He lives at the Glass Lantern Tavern, Plough Yard in Grays Inn Lane

He gives his opinion for nothing

Plague pottiness

Doctors said that dogs and cats, pigs, pet rabbits and pigeons could spread the plague. The government believed them and tried to prevent the plague by killing all the dogs in the town. Dogs were banned from towns and dog-killers were appointed to round up strays.

Other doctors blamed dirty air – huge bonfires were lit in the hope that they would 'purify' it.

THAT'S BETTER. NICE PURE AIR

No one understood that the real enemy was the rats, whose fleas spread the plague. That fact wasn't discovered until 1898.

Other doctors offered miracle cures for the plague. They would also offer free treatment, as in the advert (left). There was a catch, of course. Doctor Kurleus would look at a plague victim and say, 'You need a quart of my medicine. That'll be three shillings please.'

'I thought your advert said you give your opinion for nothing!'

'I do,' the devious doctor would shrug. 'My opinion is free, the drink is three shillings.'

Sick people, afraid of dying a painful plague death, would give anything for a cure. The fake doctors grew rich and the people died anyway.

GUILTY!

GORGEOUS GEORGIANS

SOME OF THE MOST HORRIBLE THINGS IN HISTORY ARE THE THINGS PEOPLE DID TO THEMSELVES. WHAT THEY DID TO MAKE THEMSELVES LOOK BETTER.

Modern magazines offer readers a 'makeover' – they say they'll change someone's appearance from grot to hot in ten easy steps. If the Georgians did a makeover then the results would have been just as stunning…

1. White is beautiful, dear ladies,
   Smear your face with paint of lead;
   Never mind the lead has made
   The men who mixed it ill … or dead.

   ~ Make-up is a flat white lead paint

   YOU CAN DRAG A HORSE TO WATER BUT A FACE PAINT MUST BE LEAD

2. Take some silk of red or black,
   Cut a circle or a crescent;
   Stick it to your face to cover
   Smallpox scars … it's much more pleasant.

   ~Silk beauty spots are cut out and stuck on

   DALMATIANS ARE VERY FASHIONABLE THIS YEAR

3. Take some plaster, dyed bright red,
   Crush it to a ruby paste;
   Smear it on your lips, dear ladies,
   Never mind the chalky taste.

   ~Red Plaster of Paris is used for lips

   DON'T SMILE OR YOUR LIPS'LL DROP OFF

4. Shave your eyebrows clean away,
   Take a trap and catch some mice;
   Make false eyebrows from the mouse skin,
   Stick them on to look so nice.

   ~Black lead eyelashes and mouse-skin eyebrows are needed

   CHEESE MADAM?   YUMMY!   YES PLEASE!

5. Make your face look sweet and chubby,
   Pack your mouth with balls of cork;
   Fit your false teeth in the middle,
   Hope you don't choke when you talk.

   ~Cork balls held in the cheeks improve the face

   BUT MADAM, CRICKET BALLS ARE MADE OF CORK!

6. Next you need a monster wig
   If you want to look real smashin';
   When your wig has reached the ceiling
   Then you'll be the height of fashion!

   ~Build up the hair like a pyramid

   I'M SURE MADAM'S UMBRELLA IS IN THERE SOMEWHERE

HOW TO DRAW A GORGEOUS GEORGIAN

Martin Brown explains how to draw a Georgian lady.

YOU'LL NEED...
A SHARP PENCIL ✓
A RUBBER ✓
AN INK PEN ✓
(if you want to colour the drawing)

3

"This time we have hair – lots of it! The hair is the point of the joke here, so let's have fun with it..."

TOP TIP
Use different pencils for thicker and darker lines.

1

Martin says: "I like to use reference books, but I probably can't make the dress as silly as they were in Georgian times. The dresses went out sideways – some of them were nine feet wide!"

4

"I'll put a slight angle on the hairdo, as if it's almost falling off."

2

"I'll start with the simple box frame – even though she has a large dress on, her waist is still pulled in. A woman's hips are a bit wider."

5

"Make sure you are happy with the eyes when you are drawing. In a drawing like this everybody looks at the eyes first."

From the *Horrible Histories* Magazine

TOP TIP
Remember that Georgian dresses were symmetrical.

6

"I'm drawing a hat on this one, but Georgian ladies had everything from fruit to little models of sailing ships in their hair!"

WHAT A DEADLY DRAWING!

7

TOP TIP
Georgian women sometimes wore white lead paint in their make-up!

"Use the pen to add a little depth to the dress, then you can rub out the pencil lines."

8

"There you have it! Those dresses really were ridiculous. How did they even sit down?"

VILE VILLAINS

The Georgians had some pretty famous villains. The trouble is they became heroes, a bit like Robin Hood.

Take smugglers, for example. Georgian Britain was a time for smuggling. Lots of people seemed to think they were doing a good job – half the tea drunk in Britain was smuggled in to the country. Lace was smuggled in – stuffed inside geese; brandy kegs were hidden inside lobster pots; tobacco was twisted into ropes and hidden amongst the ropes used on the ships.

All good fun and part of the game called 'cheat-the-government'. Smugglers today are seen as brave outlaws.

The trouble was these 'brave outlaws' were just nasty, cruel and greedy. They'd probably cut your throat just for the fun of it and then say, 'You still think I'm a hero?'

Here is the terrible truth about one of these 'exciting' criminals.

THE HIGHWAYMAN

Name: Dick Turpin (also called himself John Palmer)
Claim to fame: Highwayman
Life: 1705 – 1739

The story:
• Brave and handsome hero who was a wonderful rider.
• He robbed stage coaches but was always very polite ... especially to ladies.
• He rode his gallant horse, Black Bess, all the way from Essex to York in record time to prove he couldn't have committed a crime ... though he had.

The terrible truth:
• He was a butcher boy till he decided there was more money in stealing cattle than chopping them. He joined 'The Essex Gang' of violent house-breakers. They entered someone's home, robbed it and tortured the occupants till they handed over their money and valuables.
• When most of the Gang was arrested Turpin tried his hand at a different crime. He stopped a gentleman on the road and threatened him with a pistol. That man was Tom King, the famous highwayman. King took Turpin as a partner. They spent two years terrorizing the Essex roads. When King was caught Turpin tried to rescue him but accidentally shot his partner dead!
• Turpin was arrested for stealing sheep in Yorkshire. No one knew he was the famous highwayman until his old teacher recognized his handwriting! Turpin ended up hanged in York. He never made the famous ride on Black Bess – though another highwayman, John Nevison, may have done.

Not to be confused with: Black Beauty, Turnip Townsend, Mashed Turnip.

WANTED

Draw a picture of yourself here.

NAME: _____

ALIAS: _____

WANTED FOR: _____

MOST HORRIBLE HABIT: _____

REWARD: _____

IT'S CRIMINAL!

TALK LIKE A PIRATE

Thinking of running away to sea on Blackbeard's boat?
If you don't want to be spotted as a lousy landlubber, learn to talk like a pirate. Here are a few words to get you started...

Ahoy 'Ahoy' means 'hello'. Most pirates aren't polite enough to use this word.

Avast ye If you see a ship you want to capture you have to tell it to stop. Do NOT shout, 'Excuse me, but would you mind slowing down so I can rob you?' Shout 'Avast ye!' It means 'Stop ... or else!'

Aye 'Yes'. You should say this to almost everything your captain asks you. Unless he asks, 'Did you steal the last of my biscuits, you bilge rat?'

Aye aye 'I'll do that right away, captain.'

Bilge The very bottom of the ship. This is where water seeps in, rats live and all the filth of the ship ends up. It stinks and the air down there is deadly. Never call a pirate a 'bilge rat' or he may take a cutlass to your cheeky tongue.

Hairy Willy Dried fish. It might look disgusting, but it's better than nothing ... just remember you're eating something pirates call 'Hairy Willy'.

Heave to Want a ship to stop? Then call out 'heave to' – that means 'stand still'. It has nothing to do with 'heaving overboard', which is what you'd do if you found an enemy on your ship.

Landlubber A 'lubber' is a clumsy person on a ship, who'd be happier on land. If you really want a cutlass up your nose, call a pirate a 'landlubber'.

Scurvy knave 'Scurvy' means despicable, nasty and generally rotten or scabby. And a 'knave' is a villain. So scurvy knave or scabby villain: take your pick – or pick your scab.

Scuttle If you're in danger from attack by another ship, you may want to sink your own ship and row off in a lifeboat. Do NOT say, 'Poke a little hole in the boat and let it sink.' To sink your own ship is to 'scuttle' it.

Shiver me timbers If a ship gets a sudden blast from a cannon then its masts ('timbers') are shaken (or 'shivered'). So a shocked ship has shivered timbers. If YOU get a shock then don't say, 'Goodness me, I am surprised!', say 'Shiver me timbers!'

Slops 'Slops' were the 1700s sailor word for trousers. Sailors were among the first people to wear them.

Swabbie A 'swab' was a mop made of rope ends or threads. A 'swabbie' had the job of mopping the deck – cleaning up the blood and guts after a fight.

SPOT THE LOT!

Can you spot ten differences between these two pictures of beastly Blackbeard? Answers at the back of the bookazine.

DRAW YOUR OWN PIRATE FLAG

Everybody knows pirates flew skull-and-crossbone flags

But did you know that flags often had bleeding hearts or daggers or whole skeletons on them? Black Bart designed his own flag, showing a giant figure of himself standing, sword in hand, astride two skulls labelled ABH ('A Barbadian's Head') and AMH ('A Martinican's Head').

Calico Jack

Blackbeard

Black Bart

Henry Every

Thomas Tew

Stede Bonnet

PUTRID PIRATE BATTLE SHIPS

Challenge your mate to a game of Putrid Pirate Battleships and see who ends up in Davey Jones's Locker first...

HOW TO PLAY

1. Pull out, copy or photocopy the page opposite and give two grids, A and B, and a pencil to each player. You'll mark the position of your own ships on grid A, and track where your enemies ships are on grid B.

2. Mark the position of your ships on grid A. You have five different ships to add, and they're all different sizes – have a look at the Pirate Ship Chart. Make sure your enemy can't see where you've put your ships!

3. Take turns to fire at each other by guessing the coordinates of your enemy's ships. When the other player guesses a square where part of one of your ships is, shout 'Hit!' When they guess a square where you don't have a ship, shout 'Miss!'

4. Mark a hit on grid B with an 'X' in the square. Mark a miss on grid B with an 'O' in the square.

5. Shout out 'Sunk!' when one of your ships has been completely sunk.

6. The winner is the player to sink all of their enemy's ships first!

SHIP	Cruiser	Battleship	Galleon	Schooner	Life raft
NUMBER OF SQUARES	5	4	3	3	1

A

	1	2	3	4	5	6	7	8	9	10
A										
B										
C										
D										
E										
F										
G										
H										
I										
J										

B

	1	2	3	4	5	6	7	8	9	10
A										
B										
C										
D										
E										
F										
G										
H										
I										
J										

A

	1	2	3	4	5	6	7	8	9	10
A										
B										
C										
D										
E										
F										
G										
H										
I										
J										

B

	1	2	3	4	5	6	7	8	9	10
A										
B										
C										
D										
E										
F										
G										
H										
I										
J										

WHAT'S YOUR IDEAL JOB FROM HISTORY?

Are you a miserable miner or a secretive spy?
Take the quiz and find out!

Is lying always wrong?

I want to do something I believe in!

Would you rather work with ordinary people or do something you really believe in?

I want to work with ordinary people, like me.

Yes – I know exactly what I want to do.

You meet a boy who has stolen something to buy medicine for his sick sister. What do you do?

Do you know what you want to be when you grow up?

No – it doesn't really matter as long as I can afford to eat.

Yes!

Are you afraid of the dark?

No.

THIS JOB IS THE PITS

Which animal are you most like?

No. I lie all the time! I like pretending I'm from Russia, and wearing disguises, too.

A SPY
You're brave, brilliant, and born to serve your country. You travel into enemy territory and pass secrets back to your government. You're an ace at cracking codes, a master of disguise, and you can speak lots of different languages. But can you hold up under torture? You'll have to if your true identity is discovered…

Yes. Liars should be locked alone in their rooms and fed bread and water.

A MONK OR NUN
You're more holy than your socks! You spend your life in the monastery (or nunnery) praying, working in the fields, helping the poor and needy, praying, sleeping in an unheated room, praying, eating foul mush, and writing books. (Tip for monks – want to know how to get the bald bit on the top of your head? Rub it with a stone.)

I tell him to bring his sister to my cottage, so I can cure her.

A WISE WOMAN
You're a very important person – people who can't afford to go to the doctor come to you instead. You cure people with herbs, and use the odd magic spell. But watch out – one minute people think you're a wise woman, and the next they're calling you a witch – and the next thing you know, you're being burned at the stake!

I report him to the authorities so he can be punished. Off with his head!

AN EXECUTIONER
You've got a good aim with an axe, a strong stomach, and you look good in black. You chop the heads off criminals (and people the king or queen just don't like very much). You don't have a very popular job, but don't worry, no one knows who you are – your name is kept secret, and you wear a hood so no one can recognize you.

A crow – I've got a head for heights.

A CHIMNEY SWEEP
Your job is perfect for children – you have to be tiny to fit up the chimneys. You work in hot, dark, cramped conditions, cleaning away the soot from fireplaces, so it's too bad if you don't like small spaces or have asthma. Make sure you don't get stuck in the chimney or fall asleep on the job – your master will light a fire underneath you!

A mole – I like digging holes.

A MINER
Congratulations – you've got the dirtiest and most dangerous job of all! You work underground, digging up coal for 16 hours a day. If you think you're too young for a job like that, you're wrong – Victorian kids started working in the mines aged five. But watch out – a mining inspector said 'Mining gives more ways of dying than any other job.'

GRIM GHOSTS

In Victorian times most poor people couldn't afford to go to the theatre. So in the dim and flickering firelight of a gloomy evening, how did they entertain themselves? With stories. And what better than a ghost story. Especially if it was a true ghost story. Here is a case from Cornwall about some villainous Victorians to chill your bones colder than a tombstone in the snow...

Listen, me dears, and I'll tell you the tale of two brothers. One brother was Edmund Norway and he was a seaman. On the night of 8th February 1840 he went to bed in his cabin and fell asleep around 11 p.m. He was a thousand miles away from his home in Cornwall.

He soon had a terrible dream that made him wake up sweating and screaming. He told it to the ship's officer, Henry Wren. He said...

'I dreamed I saw my brother killed. He was riding his horse along the road from Bodmin to Wadebridge. As he rode two men attacked him, and I watched in horror as one pointed a pistol at my brother. The pistol misfired twice so they dragged him from the horse and used the pistol to club him to death before they robbed him. Then one man dragged him across the road and dropped him in a ditch. I have a terrible fear that my brother has been murdered.'

Officer Wren said, 'It was just a bad dream. Go back to sleep. We'll be home in a week and you'll see your brother is safe and sound.'

But when Edmund Norway landed there was terrible news for him. 'Your brother, Nevell, has been murdered,' they said.

The constables had made an arrest. On 13th April William Lightfoot and his brother were found guilty of murdering Nevell Norway and sentenced to hang. Before he died, William confessed.

'I met my brother at the top of Dummer Hill and we plotted to rob the next person who came along. Around 11 p.m. we saw a man riding his horse along the road from Bodmin to Wadebridge. As he rode we two attacked him. He refused to hand over his money so I pointed my pistol at him. The pistol misfired twice so we dragged him from the horse and used the pistol to club him to death before we robbed him. Then my brother dragged him across the road and dropped him in a ditch.'

How did Edmund Norway know about his brother's death a thousand miles away and sailing in an ink-black sea?
Perhaps his brother's dying spirit slipped into his dreams to say farewell? Who knows? There's nothing as mysterious as death.
So, when the night time comes, and darkness falls, go gently, my dears, and may the angels watch over you.

THE VILE VICTORIAN QUIZ

5. Use slang words.
6. Bite into your bread at dinner.
7. Call your servants 'girls'.
8. Raise your hat to a lady in the street.
9. Spit on the pavement.
10. Sit with legs crossed.

BEHAVE LIKE A VICTORIAN

If a time machine dropped your dad in Victorian London would he act like a gentleman ... or a slob? Test him with these 'do' and 'don't' problems taken from a book of Gentlemen's Manners and see if he could have been accepted by polite Victorians. Just one problem ... if he makes a single mistake he could well be frowned on for the rest of his life!

Do or don't...

1. Offer your hand to an older person to be shaken.
2. Eat from the side of your soup spoon and not the end.
3. Write to people you know on postcards.
4. Remove your overcoat before you enter someone's living room.

Want to know how to behave like a Victorian?

1. Don't. Wait until they have offered it to you.
2. Do. And remember you mustn't gurgle or suck in your breath while you sip your soup.
3. Don't. Write letters or nothing at all.
4. Do. Even if it's only a very short call.
5. Don't. Well, usually. There are some slang words that a gentleman may use. If you don't know what they are then avoid slang altogether.
6. Don't. Break off a piece and place it in your mouth.
7. Don't. Call them maids or servants.
8. Do. BUT ... wait till she has bowed to you first and do not wave your hat in the air the way the French do – put it straight back on to your head.
9. Don't. Or anywhere else for that matter!
10. Don't. The book admits that most men do this but says it is extremely impolite.

ODD ONE OUT

The 19th century was a time of great invention. There are fifteen inventions in this picture ... but only ten were first produced between 1800 and 1900, anywhere in the world. Can you spot the odd ones out and the odd ones in? Check the back of the bookazine for answers.

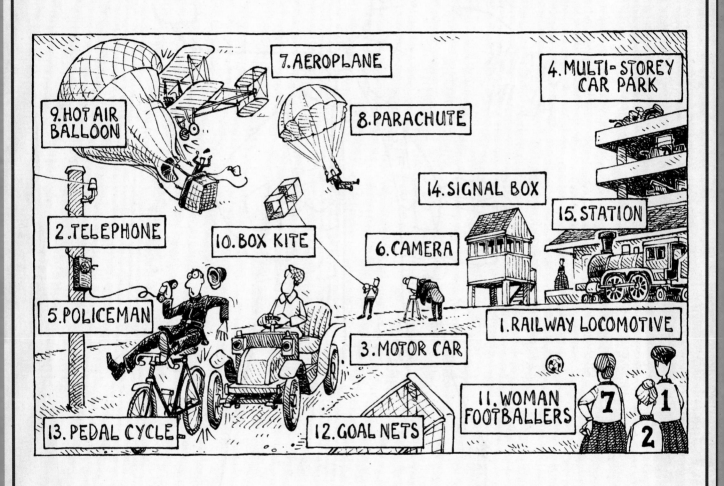

FIRST WORLD WAR FILES

FRIGHTFUL FIRST WORLD WAR

The war started in August 1914 and the soldiers were sure it would be a short sharp fight. 'One big battle and we'll win,' each side said. 'It will be over by Christmas,' the soldiers told each other. They didn't know there would be four killing Christmases before the fighting was finished. Four years of mud and blood and bullets and bombs and bitter, blinding gas. A war-weary world made a sort of peace in November 1918, and poppies and grass grew over the graves.

1914

28 June - Archduke Franz Ferdinand is assassinated in Bosnia. Austria is very annoyed because he was going to be their next emperor. (Franz is too dead to be annoyed.)

23 July - Austria blames Serbia for the death of Ferdi. Serbia grovels but apology is not accepted. This means WAR.

4 August - German army marches through Belgium to attack France, so Britain joins the war to help 'poor little Belgium'.

30 August - Meanwhile, in the east, the German army defeats the Russian army. Round one to Germany.

9 September - The French stop the Germans at the Battle of the Marne. Round two to France.

22 November - The two sides have battered one another to a standstill in northern France. They dig 'trenches' opposite one another - and won't move from them much for four years.

25 December - Enemies stop fighting for a day or two, and even play friendly football matches.

1915

19 January - First Zeppelin airship bombing raids on Britain.

4 February - Germany says it will surround Britain with submarines, sink food supply ships and starve Britain to defeat.

March - British Government asks women to sign up for war work. Many do and they start doing it better than the men did!

22 April - Nasty new weapon, poisoned gas, first used against soldiers in the trenches.

7 May - German submarines sink a passenger ship, the Lusitania - on board are 128 Americans who are not even part of the war yet. Big mistake, Germany.

July - The Turkish state uses war as an excuse to wipe out an entire race of people, the Armenians. A step on the road to the terrors of the Second World War.

August - Food getting short, especially in Germany. Prices go up and taxes go up to pay for the war - £1 million a day in Britain is needed to pay for the fighting.

12 October - Nurse Edith Cavell is caught helping Brit prisoners to escape in Belgium. She says, 'If I had to, I'd do it all over again.' Germans shoot her so she can't.

1916

25 January - 'Conscription' comes to Britain. That means fit, single men have to join the army whether they like it or not.

February - The French and Germans begin the longest battle of the war, at the fortress of Verdun in north-eastern France. Even Big Bertha (that's a gun firing one-ton shells, not a woman) can't win it for the Germans.

March - German soldiers are told to have one day a week without food to save on supplies – but the officers seem to eat well every day!

31 May - The only great sea battle of the war takes place at Jutland. Germans claim victory but never try to fight the Brit navy again.

1 July - The Battle of the Somme begins. Today Brits outnumber Germans seven to one ... but lose seven men to every one German. Very bloody draw.

10 August - A frightful news film, The Battle of the Somme, is shown in Brit cinemas even though it's not over yet. It's seen by 20 million shocked Brits.

15 September - New Brit super-weapon, the 'Willie', enters the war. Luckily someone has changed its name to the 'Tank'.

18 November - End of the Battle of the Somme.

1917

January - A munitions factory blows up in Silvertown, East London, killing 73.

February - The Russian people rebel against their leaders and Russian soldiers lend their rifles to help the revolution. Good news for Germany.

April - The Doughboys are here! No, not bakers' men, but American soldiers as the USA joins the war. Meanwhile French troops rebel against their conditions.

June - Brit ban on rice being thrown at weddings and feeding birds – food is too precious.

July - The war now costs Britain nearly £6 million a day. Will they run out of money or men first?

1 August - Terrific rain storms as the British attack in Flanders. The mud is as deadly an enemy as the Germans.

September - German submarines shell Scarborough.

October - Brit bakers allowed to add potato flour to bread while French bread has become grey, soggy stuff.

6 December - German Giants reach London. (They're bomber aircraft, not monster men.) They're harder to catch than the old Zeppelins.

1918

January - Britain is forced to have two meatless days a week and no meat for breakfast. Shops with margarine are raided by desperate women!

21 March - Called the 'last day of trench warfare'. The Germans break out and smash the Allies back from the trenches.

1 April - The Royal Air Force is formed and celebrate by shooting down German ace von Richthofen – the Red Baron – three weeks later.

June - 30 people die in Lancashire. They had Spanish flu. No one has any idea how many millions it's about to kill. Far more than the war, for sure.

July - At the Marne River the Allies stop retreating. The tide is turning back towards Germany. The Russian rebels massacre their royal family.

8 August - German General Ludendorff calls this 'the black day of the German army' as they are driven back. Still, no one expects the war to end this year.

October - German sailors are ordered to make one great last voyage to destroy the Brit fleet – or be destroyed. Sailors refuse and pour water on their ships' boiler fires.

9 November - Kaiser Wilhelm is thrown out of Germany. He retires to Belgium. After what he did to them four years ago it's not surprising they don't want him! He ends up in Holland.

11 November - Armistice Day and peace is agreed at last. The peace document is signed at the 11th hour of this 11th day of the 11th month.

LEARN THE LINGO

Every soldier needs to talk soldier language. Learn these and your sergeant will test you on them tomorrow!

ALLEY Go! Clear out! Run away! From French 'allez'.

BUMF Toilet paper, or newspaper used for the toilet. Later on it came to mean any useless letters from the army. From bum-fodder, a 1700s word.

CANTEEN MEDALS Beer or food stains on the front of your tunic.

CHARPOY Bed. From the Hindustani word.

CHAT A louse.

CHINSTRAPPED Tired, exhausted. The idea is a man can be so tired he is held upright only by the chinstrap of his cap or helmet. (It's a joke.) In fact chinstraps are used only by troops on horseback. Other soldiers think that if a bullet hits their helmet, the chinstrap may choke them or break their jaw.

COLD MEAT TICKET A disc worn around the neck. Men are given red and green discs. These give the name and number of the soldier. If he is killed, one disc stays with the body (the cold meat).

DAISIES Boots. From Cockney rhyming slang 'daisy roots'.

DEVIL DODGER Army priest.

FLEABAG Sleeping bag.

GOGGLE-EYED BOOGER WITH THE TIT British gas helmet. The wearer has to breathe in through his nose and breathe out through a valve held in his teeth.

JAKES Latrines. Expression dating back to Elizabethan times.

KILTIE A Scottish soldier.

KNUT A person (usually an officer) who is fussy about how they look. The word comes from the popular music-hall song by Arthur Wimperis (1874-1953) Gilbert the Filbert, the Colonel of the Knuts.

LANDOWNER A dead man. To 'become a landowner' was to be dead and buried.

QUICK FIRER A postcard. The card has sentences printed which can be crossed out to give your message. E.g. 'I am/am not fit/dead and hope to be home soon/next year/in a box'.

RATS AFTER MOULDY CHEESE (RAMC) Doctors and nurses ... the Royal Army Medical Corps.

REST CAMP A cemetery.

THIRD MAN To go too far into danger. This is from a story that an enemy sniper can see a match struck at night. Light a second man's cigarette after your own and the sniper has time to take aim ... light the third man's and the sniper fires. The second man is fine – the third man is one too far.

ENEMY GENERALS

Copy the Trench Rat into the squares.

Terrible Trench Toilets

The British dig trenches in the ground so they are safe from enemy bullets and can attack. The enemy sit in their trenches to defend. The French and British build simple trenches because they don't plan to stay there. They are always wanting to attack. The Germans build solid and clever trenches. They use concrete and have dugouts deep underground.

There are no proper toilets in most of the Brit trenches, just buckets. If you upset the sergeant then you may be given the job of taking the buckets out after dark. Your job is to dig a hole and empty the buckets.

DID YOU KNOW?
A soldier usually makes over a kilo of poo and pee each day. In an army company in the trenches this is a ton a week.

NAME THAT WEAPON

If you are going into battle you will need to carry a lot of stuff. The army gives you weapons (usually a bayonet and a rifle) but many soldiers use extra special ones too...

BAYONET

A long knife fastened to the end of your rifle. Used to stab the enemy to death when you haven't time to fire. Invented in France in the 1600s.
For: Good for slicing bread, opening cans, scraping mud off uniforms, poking a trench fire or digging toilet pits.
Against: You can have someone's eye out if you're not careful. And if you stick it in the enemy you may have trouble pulling it out again!

KNUCKLEDUSTERS

Wrap these around your fingers.
For: If you are hand-to-hand with a German soldier, and you have run out of bullets, these will help you smash his teeth in or put out his eyes ... if he doesn't get you first!
Against: Another heavy thing to carry and not much good if your enemy still has a loaded gun.

HAND GRENADE

Hand grenades are bombs you can throw – but in the First World War they can be deadly ... for the thrower! There are accidents every day.
For: They are thrown by hand...
Against: ...But you can only throw them about 30 metres. At 30 metres your enemy can shoot you. Oh, dear. So some soldiers invent grenades with handles. The hair brush (or racket) grenade was a paddle-shaped piece of wood with a tin box fastened to it. Steel plates in the box are flung out when it explodes and rip into enemy bodies and faces.
It's a bit hard to get the throwing right. Some soldiers have catapults. Elastic Y-shaped ones (like they used at school).
A sports shop in London, Gamages, makes one that fires grenades 150 metres. Sadly the rubber soon goes rotten. If it snaps as you let go the grenade lands at your feet. Oooops!

MAXIM MACHINE GUN

A gun that fires off a stream of bullets, around 10 bullets every second.
For: One machine gun is said to be worth around 80 rifles. Good for defending your trench.
Against: The Maxim weighs 62kg and needs to rest on a stand. It gets hot very quickly and bullets can jam. The British army is not keen on them in 1914 and only have a few hundred. The Germans have 12,000 at the start of the War and 100,000 by the end.

SPRING GUN

Captain West invented the spring gun. It is a cross between the Roman ballista and the medieval French trebuchet.

For: Can throw bombs up to 250 metres. It's still as dangerous as the hand-held ones.

Against: It has to be carried through the trenches by two men and if it fails then the bomb drops at your own feet.

SHARP SPADE

Many soldiers use a short-handled spade (or 'entrenching tool') fastened to their bayonet.

For: You can sharpen the blade so that it's just as deadly as a bayonet. These tools could then be used to 'dig in' after soldiers had taken a trench.

Against: Very clumsy to carry. It can trip you up or get caught in the barbed wire.

TANKS

These machines can move forward through mud. The soldiers on foot can walk behind and shelter from enemy bullets.

For: Good shields. Scare the enemy who often run away when they see them.

Against: They break down, and get stuck in the mud. Worst of all is if you're trapped inside when they catch fire.

CRICKET BALL GRENADE

A little bomb like a cricket ball with a handle. Strike the ball like a match then throw it.

For: Some other grenades explode at your feet if you drop them, but not this one. The Germans aren't very good at cricket so they can't bat it back.

Against: If the ball or the box get wet they won't work. If you can't throw a cricket ball you're not much use throwing this!

TANKS A LOT!

ZEPPELINS

A Zeppelin is a gas-filled balloon with a motor to take it where you want to go.

On 19 January 1915 the Germans make the first Zeppelin airship raids to drop bombs on Britain – on Great Yarmouth and King's Lynn on the east coast. On 7 June 1915 the first Zeppelin airship is shot down over Flanders, northern France.

For: They can drop firebombs from a few hundred metres up, and kill over 500 people during the War. They can't aim well so this includes women and children, cats and dogs.

Against: That slow-moving bag of gas makes a Zeppelin an easy target for an enemy fighter plane. And they burn fiercely.

DID YOU KNOW...?

A Zeppelin is shot down over London and a reporter goes to see where it has crashed in flames. He writes...

The crew numbered nineteen. One body was found in the field some way from the wreckage. He must have jumped from the doomed airship from a great height. So great was the force with which he struck the ground that I saw the print of his body clearly in the grass. There was a round hole for the head, then deep marks of the body, with outstretched arms, and finally the legs wide apart. Life was in him when he was picked up, but the spark soon went out. He was, in fact, the commander of the airship.

LIFE ON THE HOME FRONT

DAFT DORA

Who was DORA? DORA was Britain's Defence of the Realm Act. And DORA could be very fussy.
The people of Britain had to live by DORA's rules. But which rules? Here are some strange regulations. But which are real DORA rules and which are real daft rules?

DEFENCE OF THE REALM ACT

YOU MUST NOT

1 … loiter under a railway bridge
2 … send a letter overseas written in invisible ink
3 … buy binoculars without official permission
4 … fly a kite that could be used for signalling
5 … speak a foreign language on the telephone
6 … ring church bells after sundown
7 … whistle in the street after 10pm for a taxi
8 … travel alone in a railway carriage over the Forth Bridge
9 … push a handcart through the streets at night without showing a red light at the back and a white light on the front
10 … eat sweets in the classroom

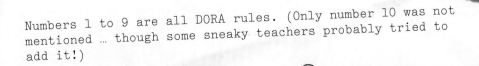

Numbers 1 to 9 are all DORA rules. (Only number 10 was not mentioned … though some sneaky teachers probably tried to add it!)

Know your enemy, they say. So if you want to survive the World War Two Blitz, get to know these blitzing bombs.

If you are close enough to spot a bomb then you'll probably be dead a few seconds later. So spot these bombs ... then duck!

High explosive

A big bang that blasts down walls, wrecks water pipes, gas pipes and electric cables and makes holes in the road so rescue vehicles can't get to the fires and the victims.

Magnesium incendiary bombs

They land and start burning fiercely. Very hard to put out the fires.

Petrol incendiary bombs

Spread flaming petrol over a wide area so there's less chance of escape.

High-explosive parachute air-mines

They float down, explode in the air and blow the roofs off buildings. That way the next lot of incendiary bombs will fall INSIDE buildings, not just on the roof tiles.

Petrol incendiary parachute air-mines

Float down and spray flaming petrol on the buildings, people, cars (and cats and dogs) below.

Flares

They float slowest of all and burn brightly. Enemy aircrafts can see them from miles away and the light shows them where to drop their bombs.

V1 flying bomb
The 'Vergeltung' 1 bomb ... and that means 'Revenge'. It flies off a sort of ski-slope launcher.

V2 rocket bomb
Bigger, faster and nastier than the V1. They go 50 miles high so there's no stopping them.

INCENDIARY BOMB

PARACHUTE AIR-MINE

V1 FLYING BOMB

V2 FLYING BOMB

DAD'S ARMY

Men over 40 who were too old to join the army in WW2 formed a Home Guard in case Hitler's army invaded Britain. They were originally known as Local Defence Volunteers, but everyone called them Dad's Army.

Some things no one tells you about Dad's Army are...

1 War starts and Dad's Army have no weapons – the real army need them. So people with guns at home hand them over... One man says he is fighting with a gun from 1880.

2 They still don't have enough weapons so they go on parade with...

Pickaxes   **Coshes**   **Spears**   **Dummy wooden rifles**

Then Winston Churchill says...

Pikes were axes on long poles used in the Middle Ages. Churchill didn't MEAN it. But someone orders metal poles with daggers on the end and a quarter of a million are made.

Dad's Army are furious ... they make them look a bit of a joke. Very few of the new 'pikes' ever leave the factory.

112

3 You may think the Nazi invaders would treat the LDV as a joke. You're wrong! When Adolf Hitler hears about Dad's Army he rants…

LDV? They are murder gangs! When we invade they will be rounded up and executed.

Dad's Army must be pleased to know Adolf is so afraid of them!

4 The LDV learn to make their own weapons. Weapons like petrol bombs.

TODAY I'M GOING TO SHOW YOU HOW TO MAKE A PETROL BOMB WITH A BEER BOTTLE AND SOME PETROL…

FIRST DRINK THE BEER … I LIKE THIS BIT…

5 Dad's Army is not all made up of older men. There are also boys too young to join the army. These fit young lads make good messengers. To make them even faster what does the LDV give the boys?

BOOM!

WHAT WENT WRONG?

HE DRANK THE PETROL

a) Motorbikes
b) Racing cycles
c) Roller skates

Answer: c) There is a Home Guard section of 'Skating Boys' who can deliver help quickly by roller-skating to the place they are called!

NO TIME TO WAIT, I'VE GOT TO SKATE!

6 Dad's Army spend a lot of time practising shooting. Some become really good shots. One soldier manages to shoot down a German bomber over London. Amazing – but true.

7 Dad's Army are a bit like Boy Scouts. The Home Guard men can earn badges if they pass tests like map-reading and first aid (which Scouts can do) … and bomb disposal (which Scouts don't do).

YOU'RE JOKING MATE! THAT'S A JOB FOR THE GIRL GUIDES!

OUT OF TIME!

The 20th century was a great hundred years for inventions. Here are 14 important 20th-century things. But how many were first made in the last century?

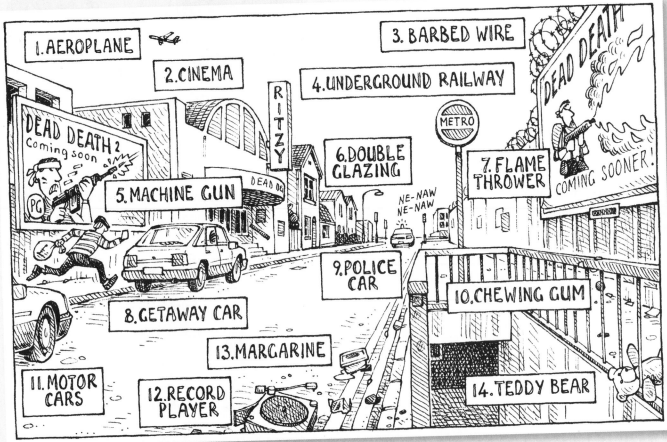

ODD ONE OUT

	RIGHT	WRONG		RIGHT	WRONG
1. Aeroplane	☐	☐	8. Getaway car	☐	☐
2. Cinema	☐	☐	9. Police car	☐	☐
3. Barbed wire	☐	☐	10. Chewing gum	☐	☐
4. Underground railway	☐	☐	11. Motor cars	☐	☐
5. Machine gun	☐	☐	12. Record player	☐	☐
6. Double glazing	☐	☐	13. Margarine	☐	☐
7. Flame-thrower	☐	☐	14. Teddy Bear	☐	☐

Answers at the back of the bookazine

GRUESOME GRID

Copy the astronaut into the squares.

AWESOME ANSWERS

Pyramid Puzzler p.15

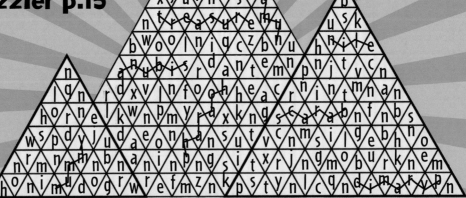

Make A Mummy p.16

D, F, J, B, A, E, H, C, I, G

Egyptian Spot the Lot p.20-21

Gruesome Greek Quiz p.24

1) Yea. At the time of the Trojan Wars, not only were children sacrificed but bits of them were eaten too. Aren't you glad you weren't around?

2) Nay. In fact they took him to the top of a cliff and threw him off. It seems a few of his stories upset them.

3) Yea. This was a popular story told by the Spartans. Of course it may have just been Spartan boasting and a big fib. But it's a warning-- don't go sticking foxes (or bears or budgies) up your jumper!

4) Nay. Draco was much tougher than that! The punishment for pinching an apple or a cabbage was death! By the way, the punishment for idleness was also death! (Think of all those dead teachers in your school if we still had that law!)

5) Yea. Peisistratus staggered into Athens bruised and bleeding and said the city would suffer if its people didn't protect him. But he had arranged the attack on himself. The people of Athens were tricked into protecting him ... even though they hated him.

6) Nay. He was sentenced to death by poisoning. And he had to drink the poison himself. Which he did. So he carried out his own death sentence. Why not ask your teacher to demonstrate how a brave teacher behaves?

7) Yea. Alcibiades was a pretty good Athenian general but switched sides to the Spartan enemies. But the Spartans didn't trust the traitor much. In the end he was murdered, shot full of Spartan arrows, and his dog would have wagged its tail in joy – if Alcibiades hadn't cut it off, that is.

8) Yea. Don't try this at home with your pet parrot. You'll make a right mess on the carpet. Stick to reading horoscopes in the newspaper.

9) Yea. She always had a pack of howling dogs with her. (If you want to carry on this ancient Greek habit then why not leave a tin of dog food at your nearest crossroads, eh? Seems a shame for Hecate to get all the grub.)

10) Nay. They painted them black with tar! They believed evil spirits would stick to the tar and be kept out. Messy.

Suffering Spartans p.24

1) Bite. Younger boys had to serve older boys. If the younger boy did something wrong he could be given a nasty nip!

2) Mountains. Babies were left up a mountain to die if they failed a health check.

3) Hair. And a bridegroom had to pretend to carry his bride off by force.

4) Beaten. Children were kept hungry and encouraged to steal food! (Spartans thought sneakiness was a handy skill in battle.) If the kids were caught stealing, they'd be beaten for being careless enough to get caught!

5) Herd. The toughest child was allowed to become leader and order the others about.

6) Baths. Stinky Spartans!

7) No clothes. So they didn't get fancy ideas about fine clothes.

8) Thistles. Children slept on beds of rushes that they gathered themselves from the river bank. In winter they could mix a few thistles in with the reeds – the prickles were supposed to give them a feeling of warmth!

9) Whipped. A horribly historical way to prove you were a good Spartan! The one who suffered the most lashes was the toughest. Some bled to death.

10) Girls. So don't mess with a Spartan miss.

The Roman Army Quiz p.32

1 b.

2 c (But they often barged straight down the middle of town streets in their chariots. They marched there too, trampling anyone who got in the way with their hob-nailed boots!)

3 a.

4 b (But they often had wives outside of the camp).

5 c.

6 b (But this rule was sometimes broken when the army was desperate for men ... and the men who were too small might still have to work for the army even if they couldn't fight).

7 a (And you'd share it with everyone else in the public toilets! Sometimes you'd use a lump of moss, though, and that would be flushed away).

8 a.

9 c.

10 b.

Quick Viking Questions p.51

1 The Danish men, women and children in Oxford were massacred. The English chopped them to bits or fried them alive in a church like Danish bacon!

2 The people of Norwich paid 'peace money' – a bribe. Of course the Vikings took the money and then robbed and destroyed Norwich anyway! Wouldn't you?

3 Ethelred had them blinded. Nasty.

4 Pray. King Ethelred ordered everyone to go barefoot to church and eat nothing but bread, water and herbs for three days. He also ordered them to pay taxes or be punished.

5 A stitch.

6 He cut bits off them – noses, ears, fingers, hands and so on. Nothing too serious.

7 Cattle bones. He was probably stunned and didn't feel the killer blow – with an axe. Dane leader Thorkeld was disgusted by the murder. Even Vikings have feelings.

8 Edmund died. Knut became king of all England.

9 He married her.

10 Fly. He stood on a tower with wings strapped to his arms, waited for a strong gust of wind, then he jumped and flapped. He got 200 metres before he crashed.

11 In battle. Forget William Shakespeare's play where Macbeth stabs Duncan in his bed – Macbeth won fair and square.

12 A poisoned one. This murder was never proved but no one was bothered one way or the other. No one liked Harthacnut anyway.

13 Three years. Shakespeare got it wrong again! In his play (with three witches) Macbeth is killed at the battle of Dunsinane.

Cutter Whey Castle p.56

Trapdoor Trapdoors weren't used for hanging people until the 1800s. Instead the victim was sent up a ladder and the ladder was taken away.

Fork They used knives, spoons and fingers, but forks weren't used until the 1600s.

Toothbrush Not used in Europe until the 1600s (though the Chinese said they used them as early as 1498). Tooth cleaning was done with a cloth.

Toilet roll Invented in 1871. In the Middle Ages the posh people would use a damp cloth, the peasants would use moss or grass.

Turkey Not seen in Europe until the Spanish came across them in South America in the 1500s.

Horrible Histories First published in 1993. Imagine having to suffer history without those magnificent books! Truly horrible.

Badminton The silly sport of battering a feathered cork wasn't invented till the 1800s ... at a place called Badminton. What a coincidence!

Dentist's chair Plenty of people to pull your teeth out with pincers but the special tilting chairs weren't used till the 1800s.

Canned food Not invented till around 1800. Before that food would be steeped in salt to stop it going rotten ... or you just ate rotten food and suffered the gut-aches.

Question mark Not invented till 1580s. What do you mean, 'That's cheating'? Oh come on – this is a *Horrible Histories* quiz!

Red herrings: glasses, clock, lighthouse, fireworks, playing cards, pistols, football.

Scrambled Sayings p.63

1e) 2f) 3h) 4c) 5g) 6b) 7d) 8a)

And never forget, 'A Tyrone women will never buy a rabbit without a head for fear it's a cat.'

Beastly Battle p.68-69

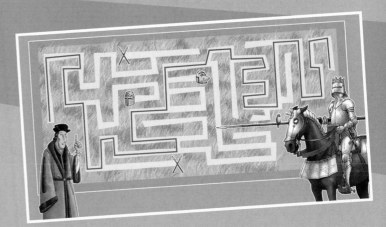

Ye Olde Tudor Wordsearch p.73

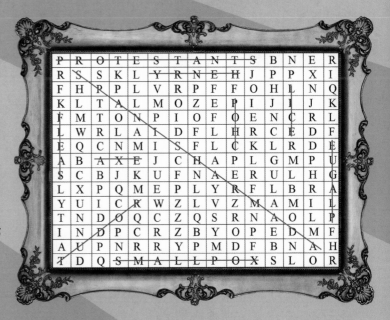

Remember, Remember...
p.76

1. True. People lit bonfires to celebrate and threw dummies on the fire dressed as Guy Fawkes.

2. True. The first record of this was at Cliffe Hill in London 1606 where a dummy of the Pope joined Guy Fawkes in the flames.

3. False. Within a few years of the plot people began to use fireworks on November 5.

4. True. This village was where Guy Fawkes used to live and the people didn't think it was fair that Guy should take all the blame.

5. False. A search of the cellars is still carried out before the opening of every Parliament.

Blackbeard Spot the Lot
p.87

Odd One Out p.97

1. Railway locomotive - IN-vented in 1804 by Richard Trevithick. The Victorian age was the age of the railways with steam trains crossing the country. The first railway death was in 1828, when driver John Gillespie's boiler blew up on the famous Stockton and Darlington railway.

2. Telephone - IN-vented in 1876. US inventor Alexander Graham Bell usually gets the credit for this. (Although Johann Reis of Germany did show a telephone device in 1860 made of a violin case and a sausage skin!)

3. Motor car - IN-vented in France in 1862. The 19th century also saw the first road death (London, 1896), drunken driver (London, 1897), car theft (Paris, 1896) and speeding motorist (Kent, 1896).

4. Multi-storey car park - OUT... but only just. In May 1901 an electric carriage company built a 7-storey garage for its vehicles.

5. Policeman - OUT. The London police force was created in 1829 but the world's first was in Paris in 1667.

6. Camera - IN-vented in the 1830s.

7. Aeroplane - OUT. Orville Wright made the first powered heavier-than-air flight in 1903.

8. Parachute - OUT because the first jump was made from a hot-air balloon in 1797. You can be excused for getting this one wrong because the first jump in Britain was in 1802 and the first jump by a British person (who lived) was in 1838. The year before a Brit died trying.

9. Hot-air balloon - OUT. First flight made in 1783 near Paris.

10. Box kite - IN-vented in Australia, 1893.

11. Woman footballers - IN-vented in 1895 by Lady Florence Dixie who formed the British Women's Football Club.

12. Goal nets - IN-vented by a Liverpool engineer in 1890.

13. Pedal cycle - IN-vented in Scotland in 1839.

14. Signal box - IN-vented in London, 1839.

15. Station - IN-vented in Baltimore, USA in 1830.

Out of Time! p.115

1 Aeroplane - Yes. First powered heavier-than-air flight in USA, 1903.

2 Cinema - No. New Orleans 1896.

3 Barbed wire - No. 1867.

4 Underground railway - No. 1870.

5 Machine gun - No. First used in war in 1879.

6 Double glazing - No. England, 1874.

7 Flame-thrower - Yes. Gas-powered machine invented in Berlin, 1900.

8 Getaway car - Yes. Three Paris shop-robbers used one in 1901.

9 Police car - Yes. USA, 1903. (Two years after the first criminals used a car! A bit late!)

10 Chewing gum - No. 1872.

11 Motor cars - No. First petrol car 1883.

12 Record player - No. 1879.

13 Margarine - No. 1869.

14 Teddy Bear - Yes. 1902 but the USA and Germany still argue over who had the first teddy.

AWFUL INDEX

ALSO AVAILABLE

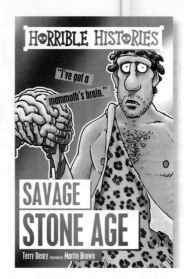

HORRIBLE HISTORIES

"I've got a mammoth's brain."

SAVAGE STONE AGE

Terry Deary Illustrated by Martin Brown

HORRIBLE HISTORIES

"Tomb service."

AWESOME EGYPTIANS

Terry Deary & Peter Hepplewhite Illustrated by Martin Brown

HORRIBLE HISTORIES

"It's all Greek to me!"

GROOVY GREEKS

Terry Deary Illustrated by Martin Brown

HORRIBLE HISTORIES

"It's got the axe-factor!"

VICIOUS VIKINGS

Terry Deary Illustrated by Martin Brown

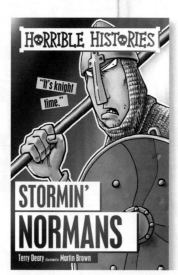

HORRIBLE HISTORIES

"It's knight time."

STORMIN' NORMANS

Terry Deary Illustrated by Martin Brown

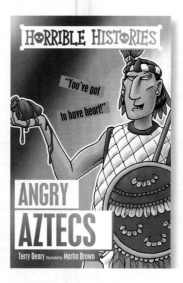

HORRIBLE HISTORIES

"You've got to have heart!"

ANGRY AZTECS

Terry Deary Illustrated by Martin Brown

HORRIBLE HISTORIES

"Inca stinka"

INCREDIBLE INCAS

Terry Deary Illustrated by Martin Brown & Philip Reeve

HORRIBLE HISTORIES

"Very amusing!"

VILE VICTORIANS

Terry Deary Illustrated by Martin Brown

HORRIBLE HISTORIES

"I'm going up in the world."

VILLAINOUS VICTORIANS

Terry Deary Illustrated by Martin Brown

HORRIBLE HISTORIES

"Cruel Britannia."

BARMY BRITISH EMPIRE

Terry Deary Illustrated by Martin Brown

HORRIBLE HISTORIES

"I get the point!"

OTTEN ROMANS

Deary Illustrated by Martin Brown

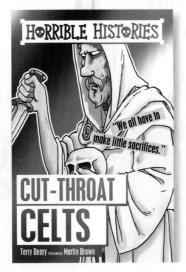

HORRIBLE HISTORIES

"We all have to make little sacrifices."

CUT-THROAT CELTS

Terry Deary Illustrated by Martin Brown

HORRIBLE HISTORIES

"Bloomin marvellous."

SMASHING SAXONS

Terry Deary Illustrated by Martin Brown

HORRIBLE HISTORIES

"Knight knight!"

EASLY MIDDLE AGES

y Deary Illustrated by Martin Brown

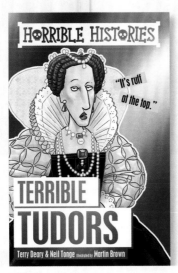

HORRIBLE HISTORIES

"It's ruff at the top."

TERRIBLE TUDORS

Terry Deary & Neil Tonge Illustrated by Martin Brown

HORRIBLE HISTORIES

"Penny for the guy!"

SLIMY STUARTS

Terry Deary Illustrated by Martin Brown

HORRIBLE HISTORIES

"Big wig."

GORGEOUS GEORGIANS

Terry Deary Illustrated by Martin Brown

HORRIBLE HISTORIES

"There's a stench n the trench."

RIGHTFUL FIRST WORLD WAR

y Deary Illustrated by Martin Brown

HORRIBLE HISTORIES

"Tanks a lot."

WOEFUL SECOND WORLD WAR

Terry Deary Illustrated by Martin Brown

HORRIBLE HISTORIES

"The Blitz is the pits!"

BLITZED BRITS

Terry Deary Illustrated by Martin Brown & Kate Sheppard

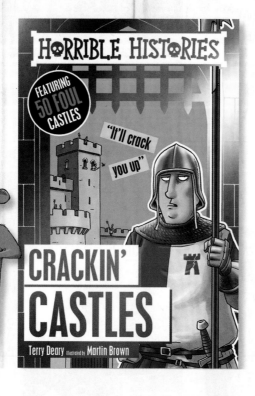

HORRIBLE HISTORIES

FEATURING 50 FOUL CASTLES

"It'll crack you up"

CRACKIN' CASTLES

Terry Deary Illustrated by Martin Brown

HORRIBLE HISTORIES

THIS IS A HORRIBLE JOURNAL

MAKE YOUR OWN HORRIBLE HISTORY EVERY DAY!

Terry Deary
Illustrated by Martin Brown

COMING SOON

HORRIBLE HISTORIES

"Daddy was a baddy."

CRUEL KINGS AND MEAN QUEENS

Terry Deary

HORRIBLE HISTORIES

"Alive alive

oh!"

GRUESOME GUIDE TO DUBLIN

Terry Deary

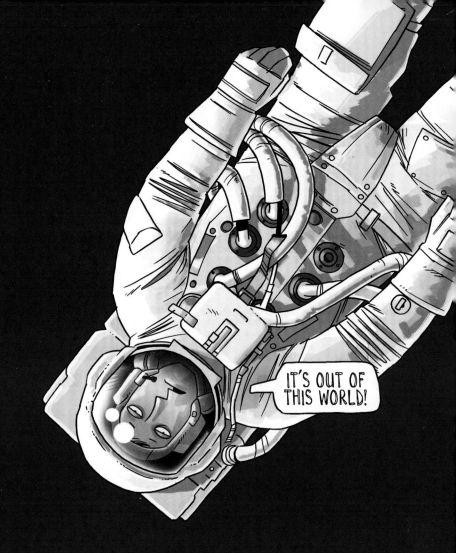